UFO QUEST

In Search of the Mystery Machines

Alan Watts

BLANDFORD

A BLANDFORD BOOK

First published in the UK 1994 by Blandford
A Cassell Imprint
Cassell plc, Wellington House
125 Strand, London WC2R 0BB

Text copyright © 1994 Alan Watts
Reprinted 1995

Distributed in the United States by Sterling Publishing Co., Inc.,
387 Park Avenue South, New York, NY 10016-8810

Distributed in Australia by Capricorn Link (Australia) Pty Ltd,
2/13 Carrington Road, Castle Hill, NSW 2154

British Library Cataloguing-in-Publication Data
A catalogue entry for this title is available from the British
Library

ISBN 0-7137-2449-8

Typeset by Litho Link Ltd, Welshpool, Wales, UK
Printed and bound in Great Britain by
Biddles Ltd, Guildford and King's Lynn

Contents

Acknowledgements

When you create a book using so many sources of information it is inevitable that some people you should have thanked are forgotten. However, I would like to thank specially: Leonard Cramp for his willing permission to quote from his work and reproduce some of his diagrams; also Ron West of the Essex UFO Research Group for permission to use some of his research into crop designs in East Anglia; Pat Delgado for the photograph of the Cheesefoot Head circles; and Catherine Birch for permission to use her mother's letter.

Then there is my indebtedness to Mavis Burrows of the Hadleigh Healing Centre for giving me the rare opportunity of studying and reproducing what may well be drawings from another planet. The Johnson family of Brightlingsea, Essex, helped a great deal through long discussions on aspects of this work and introduced me to books I had not, up to then, seen. They then read the manuscript as lay members of the public.

Studying UFOs is like looking on to a dark film set where you do not know the script or the nature of the actors. Now and again a strange new apparition appears to make you wonder. It may make an already hazy notion of what is going on even more obscure or it may produce some measure of enlightenment. My thanks to the many free spirits who have tried to record the often weird manifestations of these curious phenomena and have written about them in a multitude of books. This way some enlightenment has come and, I hope that, while I know many of my ideas will not survive the test of time, this book will add to the cause of enlightenment rather than obscuration.

Introduction: Early Days

It was Desmond Leslie and George Adamski who initially made me aware of UFOs with their book *Flying Saucers Have Landed* (1953). Though not quite the first work on the subject, it was the first one I'd read and, like many others, I found I had a wide chasm of doubt to cross before I could accept the reality of these objects. Yet by gathering so much evidence, Leslie and Adamski had, logic decreed, shown that here was a mystery worth investigating.

From Desmond Leslie I learned that the history of flying saucers did not start on 24 June 1947 – the day Kenneth Arnold landed and reported that his light aircraft had been buzzed near Mount Rainier by a formation of nine disc-shaped objects, travelling, he estimated, at some 1,500 m.p.h. An avid press lapped up the story of such out-of-this-world craft, 'skipping along like saucers', and the modern wave of flying-saucer sightings was born.

Why this particular event hit the headlines so forcibly across the USA is difficult to say, for Arnold was not the first to give these craft the appellation 'saucers'. The *Denison Daily News* for 25 January 1878 reported that a Texas farmer, John Martin, saw a 'dark flying object' in the shape of a disc cruising high in the sky at 'wonderful speed', and he used the word 'saucer' to describe it. Probably plenty of others who have never got into print have done exactly the same thing over many, many years – at least since saucers were married to cups.

The word 'saucer' is so descriptive of most alien spacecraft seen in the skies of the world that it is the accepted term wherever you go. However, now we are forced to use the US Air Force term 'Unidentified Flying Object' (UFO). This came into use because the authorities wanted to distinguish between alien objects and the terrestrial planes, rockets, spacecraft, etc. that they could actually identify on their radars. As there were plenty of weird shapes other than saucers to be seen, the flying saucers became UFOs to all those in the unofficial research groups that sprang up across the world.

These groups did, and still do, a very important job, continuing to publish the details of sightings and contacts in the face of stone-walling tactics from the military authorities. The latter have always sought information about UFOs, but individuals who, in their innocence, handed over precious documentation and photographs would find that somehow these had been lost, mislaid or inadvertently destroyed.

Threatened with the official secrets acts, air-force personnel, and even airline pilots, have found themselves unable to tell of their close encounters with out-of-this-world spacecraft which flew alongside the wing-tips of them. It was only the vigilance and persistence of groups like the American Aerial Phenomena Research Organization (APRO) and the National Investigation Commission on Aerial Phenomena (NICAP), as well as the British Unidentified Flying Object Research Association (BUFORA) and similar bodies of dedicated enthusiasts in other countries, which saved many of the most convincing sightings for the rest of us to study; these and the several US Air Force officers who, faced with a life of telling lies about objects the existence of which they were ordered to deny, wrote books on the subject once they were clear of their official entanglements – people like E. J. Ruppelt, Donald Keyhoe and Alan Hynek.

However, I cannot wholeheartedly condemn the military authorities for their debunking stance. In their position, faced with a perceived aerial 'threat' over which they had no control, I feel I would have done the same. You have only to imagine the furore that would have followed the President of the United States going on air to tell the world that we were being visited by spacecraft from places of which we had no knowledge to see the dilemma that the security forces were in. If he had added that the most advanced air-force fighters would be powerless against these craft should they decide to turn hostile, then the political repercussions would have been incalculable.

I joined the most prestigious of the British groups as soon as I could. This was the then London Unidentified Flying Object Research Organization (LUFORO), which very soon expanded its brief to include the whole country and became BUFORA. By this time I was quite convinced that we were dealing with an advanced but nevertheless technological set of machines, and several of us who were like-minded and had had a scientific training formed an inner conclave. We wanted a nuts-and-bolts description of the saucer and we wanted, in the face of much high-flown pseudo-scientific waffle, to keep our feet firmly on the ground. To this end we decided to concentrate on one form of saucer of which we had good pictures. This was the device that George Adamski had photographed near his home on the slopes of Mount Palomar and had included in *Flying Saucers Have Landed* (1953).

Some people were already thinking deeply about the saucer as a piece of advanced engineering. One such was Leonard Cramp, an aeronautical engineer from the Isle of Wight. He set down his ideas in a book called *Space, Gravity and the Flying Saucer* (1954), which had a profound effect on me and my subsequent thinking about the saucer's form of propulsion. Cramp took the best evidence available and analysed it as something that had to be engineered: he made cutaway drawings of what Adamski's saucer ought to look like inside and how its shell ought to be fabricated.

None of us took Adamski's pictures at face value but, as described in Chapter 4, a schoolboy photographed Adamski's saucer again in England and Cramp was able to show, by orthographic projection, that this was identical to Adamski's original. We now had something which was repeatable and this increased our confidence enormously.

Then some startling things happened. We got hold of bits of a strange 'space toy' that had fallen in a remote part of Yorkshire. When the materials of which it was made were scientifically analysed, they were found to be of such extreme purity and of such complex construction that any hoaxer would have needed resources well in advance of the technology of the day. Amazingly, the construction of the so-called Silpho Moor object looked uncannily like parts of the drawing that Cramp had made of the 35-ft-diameter Adamski saucer.

These events, together with continuing reports of the curious way in which saucers were interfering with the ignition systems of cars, all began to lead me to an idea of how the saucer might be propelled. I was elated to find, when I did the sums on my theory, that they produced the right orders of magnitude for the kind of magnetic aura that could be broadcast by a saucer and interfere with a car's electrics. The chance discovery of some physics ideas on the frontiers of knowledge began to explain certain curious aspects of UFO behaviour that had up till then made people doubt the evidence of their own eyes. I published some of this work in a UFO journal (Watts, 1962), but already the knockers were moving in.

In the succeeding years pseudo-scientists came to dominate many of the UFO organizations. Even though no one knew just what we were dealing with, we often got reports edited through the limited knowledge of those who wrote them up. Others set themselves up to 'evaluate' the reports and so were able to dismiss sightings which did not fit in with their own view of what was and what was not a genuine UFO. Often at this time I felt that maybe the powers-that-were had managed to infiltrate the UFO organizations with their own agents, so wrecking our efforts from the inside. In retrospect, I do not think they did; they did not need to, as there were plenty of power-seekers ready to do the job for them.

Thus several of us who had set out in the early days with high hopes of understanding at least part of the phenomenon eventually withdrew into our little private shells and let the amateur psychologists and self-professed scientists talk round the subject until many had convinced themselves that craft which acted so strangely could not possibly be real.

Maybe we would never have got the answers to any of the questions we posed ourselves, but this book tells (among other things) how a series of interesting coincidences led to one of our number putting together a theory to explain how an Adamski-type saucer propelled itelf. He now realizes that he has only a part of the answer – and a small part at that. However, the theory does begin to make sense of some of the strange things which lead so many people to doubt the objective reality of UFOs.

One of the greatest UFOs of them all is the immense space 'airship' which Jacques Vallée christened a 'cloud-cigar', because of its shape and the way it wraps wreaths of what looks like vapour round itself. If there is one constant feature of the UFO phenomenon, it is that these great craft act as 'aircraft-carriers' for the smaller saucers, and whenever a wave of saucer sightings occurs you should look around for the 'cloud-cigar' that has brought them. When you have seen this great aerial 'submarine', as I have on more than one occasion, you realize that the saucer denizens, while more advanced than us technologically, still need to transport their smaller craft in carriers, just as we do when we have to move a task force to some potential or actual theatre of operations.

So, while there are aspects of the UFO saga that seem to defy logic, I believe that many odd UFO sightings can be explained. Not all of them, but a fair number. Modern physics gives us possible answers to the way these things move and to how they can seem to disappear or distort their images, so that they look like something else. The craft may even be able to make themselves invisible at the same time as revealing their solidity by the big blips that form on our radar screens.

However, our best approach is to let often incredulous witnesses tell their stories and maybe lead us towards the truth. This way we will move from twentieth-century physics into a world which might well become twenty-first-century technology. Before we can attempt to become one of the space races, we must move forward on many fronts, not the least of which is an acceptance of the psychological superiority of those who are visiting us.

Through my own investigations into the wonderful crop designs that have appeared in our fields over the last decade, I have come into contact with a psychic lady who, without the benefit of any art training, has involuntarily become the recipient of some thirty-five 'canvases' of what I can only describe as 'space-art'. Unbeknown to her at the time, there were depictions of UFOs among the welter of strange devices that populated her drawings and she has been 'told' that this bequest has 'something to do with crop circles'. We will describe this and other mysteries in the final chapters.

Note

Converting Imperial measurements to metric

Throughout this book measurements are mainly given in Imperial. Those readers who are more familiar with metric might find the following useful:

To convert in to cm: × 2.54
(e.g. 2 in = 5.08 cm)

To convert ft to m: × 0.30

To convert yd to m: × 0.91

To convert miles to km: × 1.60

To convert oz to g: × 28.34

To convert lb to g: × 453.60

The Coming of the New Age

For the first time in maybe 2,000 years a new age is upon us. We see its manifestations whenever we pick up a book or magazine discussing evidence for mysterious goings-on on earth and in the sky. I believe that this will be an age of meaningful communication between space races and ourselves, for there is ample evidence that as our awareness of technology and outer space increases, so also do the examples of forms of communication from intelligences beyond this planet. The modern manifestations of pictograms (crop circles) in our fields and their developing sophistication are important examples.

While the evidence for aerial craft visiting earth goes back as far as recorded history – and further if cave paintings etc. are taken into account – the modern wave of UFO sightings suggests that it is human beings' acquisition of advanced technology which has spawned a probably unprecedented interest in us and our welfare by space races from many different parts of the galaxy.

The evidence for spacecraft and their denizens arriving on our soil and entering our oceans is now so totally overwhelming that no one can doubt these things are happening and have happened as far back as one cares to probe. However, things were different in the past from the way they are today. Now the average person knows what a spacecraft should look like and can give detailed technological descriptions of what he or she has seen. After all, we have done it ourselves. Not in the svelte, efficient way the saucers swim into our atmosphere without polluting it, but in the only way we know.

We can gain ideas of how these alien craft operate, but we

cannot yet emulate them. Just as we can use our computers and our best brains to fathom out how the universe began, so also will the solution to the riddle of the UFOs lie along the same painstaking path. However, we have not yet been given vital pieces of the scientific jigsaw that will allow us to emulate the saucers. We will not be able, as they do, to travel faster than light in the foreseeable future, and anyway, while our knowledge has increased tremendously in the twentieth century, we still do not have an understanding of gravity much greater than Sir Isaac Newton's, back in the 1700s.

There is a long way to go technologically before we can make a true flying saucer: developments in the 'chemistry' of fundamental matter will have to take place before we can hope to do that. For fundamental particle reactions, I believe we need to know how to make what are called in chemistry 'catalysts' (a catalyst is something that lowers the energy thresholds of reactions, allowing them to occur when otherwise they would not).

If our technology is still primitive compared to theirs, then our collective experience of contact with space denizens shows that, when it comes to control of cerebral functions, we are babies playing on the seashore of the psychological ocean. The aliens can generate amnesia in those they choose to such a degree that the victims do not know anything has happened. Only under regression hypnosis do subjects recall that they have, for instance, been taken into a spacecraft and subjected to, maybe, a form of medical examination. In some (well-researched) cases, aliens have used women whom they tagged as children as surrogate mothers, but again these unfortunates did not know what had happened to them until a hypnotist was able to extract a description of their experiences.

The space races may have been doing this kind of thing for aeons – the available evidence certainly seems to point that way – but it is only today, as we struggle towards the same degree of understanding of the world and ourselves as they possess, that they have had to contend with a civilization which answers back. Once such pychological interventions would have been put down to 'God' or 'the gods', or maybe to the ministrations of angels and demons; today the majority of us know better.

I do not think it is coincidence that the great modern wave of UFO sightings has come about after World War 2. At the end of that conflict we showed the watching space denizens what we were capable of. The atomic bombs dropped on Hiroshima and Nagasaki certainly signalled the end of the war, but they also proclaimed that *Homo sapiens* had the means of effectively destroying life on this planet. Then the inevitable development of the enormously more powerful hydrogen bomb must have left those for whom our space was more or less home in no doubt that, maybe for the second or third time in human history, we could irreparably damage our environs. We proceeded to do that with the Pacific island test of 1 November 1952, which led to the complete disappearance of Eniwetok atoll and its replacement by a crater 175 ft deep and 1 mile across. This was followed by other tests, culminating in the explosion in near space of a bomb over Johnson Island which fed so many electrified particles into earth's largely unexplored radiation belts that we shall now never know their composition before this unscientific experiment. The Johnson Island bomb resulted in aurorae over a large sector of the world, as well as highly coloured sunsets. Humans could now very effectively contaminate the UFOs' happy hunting grounds, without being able to control the power they had unleashed.

The development of our rocket programmes was closely monitored, especially by discs that flew rings round them during take-off. The Americans' much-vaunted and highly successful Apollo programme, which put men on the moon, was also closely followed and there were discs sitting on crater rims looking at the astronauts' first faltering steps into the league of space races (Wilson, 1980). There has also been, I believe, a fairly complete surveillance of earth by waves of 'scout' craft launched from the great carrier craft already mentioned. Certainly there is no part of the world that does not seem to have been visited by flying saucers and similar craft during the last fifty years or so.

I believe that this surveillance became necessary because of our development of earth satellites. The self-imposed commandment of the UFO races appears to be, 'Do what you have to do, but interfere with humans as little as possible.' They find their style cramped because the envelope of our planet has now been expanded out to 36,000 miles or more by masses of satellites in all sorts of orbits. Our own environs are now loaded with space junk, as well as functioning satellites. This means that the carrier craft always have to be on the lookout for our own spacecraft and do not have the freedom of action that they enjoyed in the 1950s, when the largest waves occurred.

However, that does not mean their interest in us and our welfare has diminished. Far from it. They are constantly finding new ways of telling us they are here. Over the years examples of writing, diagrams and drawings from races outside this planet have been received by certain often parapsychologically sensitive people. Those most likely to be the willing or unwilling recipients of space writings, etc. are people already partly tuned in to the subtler vibrations of the cosmos. It is in many ways a case of 'Seek, and ye shall find; knock and it shall be opened unto you.' Thus it was that George Adamski (who figures prominently in Chapter 4) was a contactee back in the early 1950s because he was already a person easy with the idea that space races could contact us and that, when they did, there was nothing to be afraid of. We shall discuss other contactees in later chapters.

There are many examples of odd objects that have come from UFOs, including metals with strange properties, bits of rock like pumice, as well as that curious manifestation called 'angel hair'. The number of well-attested cases of this fibrous material falling out of the sky in association with UFO sightings is great enough for there to be no doubt about its authenticity. In any case, there are photographs of people handling it, and one chemist who managed to get a specimen under the microscope described it as 'radioactive, heavily damaged cotton'. Yet angel hair cannot be kept for any length of time – it simply 'evaporates', disappearing before your eyes (Jessup, 1956). It is just another example of the ephemeral 'calling cards' left by UFOs, although there is some evidence that the military authorities in the USA have more concrete hardware kept under conditions of the very greatest secrecy (Strieber, 1990).

However, now at last the UFOs have found an unequivocal means of telling us they are here, and also of informing us of their abilities and giving us insights into what they know about us – which is a lot. I refer to the wonderful designs that are yearly being drawn in the fields of the world. What started as crop 'circles' has developed year by year until, in 1991, they formed a marvellously complex design that can be drawn only by computer and is a spin-off from one of our more modern branches of mathematics – namely, chaos theory. The appearance of the graceful heart-shaped Mandelbrot design in a field near Cambridge on 12 August (Photo 8) epitomizes the substance and the desire they have to communicate with us. They are telling us that they know our most up-to-date mathematics and can reproduce geometric designs from it on a scale of hundreds of feet and with exact precision.

Chaos theory begins to show that there is order in chaos – which the Chinese apparently knew some thousands of years ago. In this present age – called by the Brahmins the Kaliyuga, or the age of chaos – there is great need to develop order out of chaos; if we fail, maybe life as we know it will be no more. The UFOnauts that made the Mandelbrot were, some people think, trying to give us that message (Bartholomew, 1991).

This theme will be returned to again towards the end of the book. Before we get that far, though, it is worth looking at what we already know about the way the saucers operate and, using our knowledge of modern science, making some shrewd guesses as to how they achieve their wonderful performance. We may only begin to break the surface of the sea of their abilities, but it will help many people who have experienced UFO manifestations to come to terms with some of the weird things they have seen – things that make them doubt their own eyes and sometimes even lead them to feel they might be going mad. At the outset, I can assure anyone who has had a strange UFO experience that they are not going mad; it's just that the UFOs are operating in realms we are not used to. For example, when we look at something, we expect it actually to be there, in the direction we are looking. With UFOs, that may not always be the case. Certainly there is a spacecraft there somewhere, but not necessarily where you are seeing it. This is how UFOs can apparently disappear before your very eyes.

To understand such things, we need to go into some modern scientific theories. First, though, let me explain what we know about the way certain UFOs operate, and also draw on personal experience.

CHAPTER
2

Saucers and Cigars

In 1954 an unprecedented wave of UFO activity hit France. It was only part of a world-wide visitation but what made the French wave phenomenal was the sheer intensity of reports. They are covered in some detail in Jacques Vallée's *Anatomy of a Phenomenon* (1966) and of them the so-called 'Vernon cigar' is of special interest.

At about 1 a.m. on 23 August 1954, on a clear night with the moon just rising, Bernard Miserey came out of his garage, having just put away his car. He was amazed to see a huge, silent, luminous mass suspended above the river bank, about 300 yd away. He compared it to a gigantic cigar standing on end.

After a couple of minutes a horizontal disc-shaped object fell from the bottom of the cigar, came to a stop and, after swaying, dived across the river towards him, brightening as it went. When it passed over him, he could see it was surrounded by a halo of brilliant light. This disc moved away south-westwards at a 'prodigious speed' and, after a couple of minutes, another disc did the same, to be followed by two more. Eventually, after a long interval, a fifth disc came from the gigantic, motionless craft. This one dropped as low as the new bridge that had been built to replace one destroyed during the war, swaying slightly as it came to rest. It was circular and emitted a red luminosity that was most intense at the centre and faded out towards the rim. There was a glowing halo about the whole craft. After a few seconds it also wobbled, like the other four, and streaked off northwards, gaining height as it went.

During this time the 300-ft-long object had lost most of its luminosity and 'sank into darkness'. The whole amazing spectacle had lasted a full three-quarters of an hour.

What Miserey had seen – and several other reliable witnesses as well – was the carrier craft that, for want of its true name, we are going to call a Leviathan. Leviathans have been seen in earth space hundreds and hundreds of times. Sometimes the privileged observer sees the discs this 'mother ship' transports emerging. At others they are seen to re-embark, although this manoeuvre is less commonly witnessed. The reason for this seems to be that in most cases Leviathans rendezvous at altitude with their scouts but will come close to the ground to emit them when they are not likely to be threatened by terrestrial fighters.

They have always been objects which prefer altitude. For example, Aimé Michel (1957) describes the experiences of the crew of a B29 Superfortress at 18,000 ft over the Gulf of Mexico on 6 December 1952. It was 5.25 a.m. local time when the radar observer picked up the successive evolution of over half a dozen saucers from a Leviathan somewhere in their vicinity. Some of the saucers were travelling at 5,000 m.p.h. and a few flew straight at the bemused crew before flicking up past the bomber at the last possible moment. The encounter included the passage of the Leviathan itself, which crossed below them – a bluish object emitting a pale light – at such a speed that they did not have time to evaluate its exact shape. The experience ended when the radar showed the merging of the small blips with the big one, the whole group embarking into the Leviathan while the latter was travelling at around 5,000 m.p.h.

In the immediate post-war days, the performance of jet fighters was poor compared to what it is now and so the UFOnauts had greater freedom of action. Today, with high-performance jets providing a much more definite threat to the UFOs, the chances of a spectacle such as the one Bernard Miserey witnessed are very slim. Leviathans are still about, but they have to be much more circumspect in their approaches to earth; often they will be above 50,000 ft when they stop and turn up on end so they can 'fly' their saucers. For example, the Russian Tass news agency reported the monitoring of a brightly illuminated object looking like an airship that flew at an altitude of 15 miles from the Barents Sea to the Kola Peninsula on 2 September 1990 (15 miles is 80,000 ft and on the edges of space).

Also Mrs Bette Jackson of Northfield, Birmingham, saw a classic Leviathan at 12.40 a.m. on 7 March 1991 (Good, 1992). She was alerted by an 'unusual noise' and noticed that the area outside her bungalow was lit up. The source proved to be a beam of light extending downwards from a 'Zeppelin-shaped' object whose colour was light grey. She then described a classic feature of many Leviathan observations: 'The body of the object was brightly lit through what appeared to be windows' (Fig. 2.1). She describes them as square with a third white, another third amber and the remainder either red or green. Following several slow manoeuvres, which lasted some twenty-five minutes in all, and the switching off of the beam of light, the object 'simply disappeared from my view. I say this because I do not know what happened to it because I saw nothing else.' During this whole time there was a droning noise from the object which was very penetrating but lasted only about ten seconds after the light was switched off, just before the great vessel vanished in front of her eyes.

Obviously, this Leviathan was not engaged in flying off saucers, as it remained horizontally 'suspended in the air' during the long time it was probing the ground with its light. It is also possible that the craft was not a Leviathan of the kind seen by Miserey: just as terrestrial aircraft-carriers differ in shape and size, so also will these extraterrestrial space vehicles. However, it did have the 'windows', which are not, I am sure, windows at all but bright patches over the most powerful parts of the 'engines' that keep these immense craft floating just like airships but with

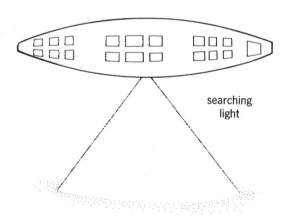

searching light

Fig. 2.1   A drawing of what Mrs Bette Jackson saw from her cottage in Northfield, Birmingham, in March 1991.

complete manoeuvrability and capable of producing immense acceleration, as personal observation (detailed in Chapter 3) testifies.

Going back to France in 1954, three weeks after the Vernon incident a Leviathan was observed in a remote country area some 250 miles south-west of Paris. This sighting has a great deal to tell us about Leviathans (Vallée, 1966). The craft emerged from what looked like a stormy layer of cloud and was first described as a 'luminous blue-violet mist of a regular shape something like a cigar or a carrot'. It came out almost horizontally but slightly tilted towards the ground and moved

> as if it were actually some gigantic machine surrounded by a mist. It descended to an altitude of about 3,000 ft, stopped and up-ended to stand vertically on end, whereupon it became motionless.
>
> All at once white smoke like a vapour trail came from the lower end of the cloud.

The trail was being sown by a small metallic disc that at first pointed to the ground but then went up to describe an ascending spiral round the mother craft. It reached the top and then descended. The disc next came down to near the ground and flew complex manoeuvres over the nearby countryside. After this it dashed in at headlong speed towards the Leviathan from about a mile out and disappeared, 'like a shooting star', into the lower end from which it had emerged. About a minute later the big craft began to turn over as it moved away and then accelerated to disappear back into the clouds in the distance. The whole observation lasted about the same length of time as many others – namely, half an hour.

Because of the 'mist' that sometimes surrounds them, these great ships have been dubbed 'cloud-cigars', and I have personally witnessed two such devices standing motionless for, in one case, hours while the swirling 'mist' made them look like flabby balloons oscillating in the wind. However, there were undeniable reasons why they could not have been balloons (see Chapter 3).

Whenever there is a wave of sightings, then associated Leviathans are almost invariably seen, as happened in the incredible series of events that rocked the military town of

Warminster in Wiltshire in 1964–5. (I mention Warminster as a military town only to help identify it; I do not believe that the events which occurred there had anything specifically to do with the presence of the Army – not that the Army was unaffected.)

The wave chose to break on Christmas Day, 1964. If the soldiers of the 1st Welch Regiment had been hoping for a lie-in on Christmas morning, then they were greatly disappointed. They were, in the event, shot from their beds by a crescendo of noise described by a sergeant '[as] if a huge chimney stack from the main block was ripped from the rooftops, then scattered in solid chunks of masonry across the whole camp area'.

That may have been what it sounded like, but there were no masonry blocks, or anything else, to be seen scattered anywhere once the cacophony died down. What the sounds were was beyond anyone's comprehension, but they certainly came from above.

Members of the 1st Welch Regiment were not the only ones to suffer trauma that morning. Imagine the sheer horror experienced by Mrs Marjorie Bye, who at 6.12 a.m. was walking to Holy Communion at Christ Church, Warminster, when she was caught in an intensity of sound that sent shock waves through her head, neck and shoulders. The barrage made her numb. The noise she described as invisible hands holding her down as it passed overhead, only letting her go when it had moved on. She was so shaken by the occurrence that she could hardly stagger from the churchyard wall, where the noise had gripped her most intensely, to the porch of the church that offered sanctuary from this devilish thing which had possessed her. It should have been a time of peace and goodwill, but this weird visitation had turned it into one of fear and apprehension.

The head postmaster of Warminster, Roger Rump, corroborated Mrs Bye's story, for in his own case it seemed as if the 5,000 tiles on his roof were being rattled about and plucked off by some tremendous force. He lived not far from the church and the time of his visitation was about the same as Mrs Bye's. Rump said that the thing, whatever it was, produced an odd humming sound, but, just as at the regimental barracks, inspection of Mr Rump's roof showed it to be as sound and intact as it had ever been.

Other testimonies from the solid citizens of Warminster showed that the noises had actually started in the night. They were the first of a wild series of events that included a flock of pigeons being killed in flight by 'sound vibrations'. All kinds of UFO phenomena carried on into 1965 – so much so that by August the local mayor called a public meeting in an attempt to allay fears. In the end, as not even the so-called UFO experts had any ideas about the source of the sounds, the meeting did not truly achieve its objective. People down there went on calling the source of the events 'the thing', although obviously a whole galaxy of individual UFOs was responsible. Among many new and unrecognizable sightings, there were some that echoed those already described. They were also pretty spectacular.

A little after 9 p.m. on the evening of 3 June 1965 a breathlessly excited lady telephoned Arthur Shuttlewood, a reporter on the local *Warminster Journal*. Mrs Patricia Phillips did this not only because she had seen a Leviathan but also because Shuttlewood had become the man you turned to when you had the latest fantastic experience to report. Shuttlewood, who knew nothing whatever about UFOs when he started, eventually wrote a book, *The Warminster Mystery* (1967), which described some of the more remarkable sightings and events of that period.

Mrs Phillips's sighting of the giant cigar-shaped UFO again lasted about the same time as the Vernon one had done – about half an hour. She described the UFO as throwing off an orange-red glow while it hung silent and vertical in the sky, without any sign of movement. There was, she said, a distinct, dark, circular patch or aperture at the base of the fiery object. At one stage a dark ring appeared round the lower end, and then the UFO turned on its axis and slid away into the void. Her son, Nigel, was able to train his small telescope on to the object and later drew a sketch which appeared in a national newspaper.

Mrs Phillips was the wife of the vicar of Heytesbury, a village 4 miles south-east of Warminster, and so her veracity was beyond question – unlike other unfortunate witnesses, who were in many cases subjected to harassment by both press and public, and had doubts cast on their sanity.

Harold Horlock and his wife, Dora, were among those not protected by the aura of sanctity surrounding a vicar and his wife, but they still told their story. They saw the same Leviathan as the Phillipses, but in some ways their testimony is more revealing, for they described it as 'two red-hot pokers hanging downwards, one on top of the other, with a black space in between' (Fig. 2.2). The red-hot pokers referred to were the garden variety, with a brilliant bulbous red and yellow head, some of which might have been flowering in the Horlocks' garden at the time. In describing this, Shuttlewood says that because of their relative positions the Phillipses and the Horlocks were obviously looking at the same object but he wonders whether there were two UFOs, one behind the other. I think not. We know that Leviathans can glow in some parts of their great bulk and not in others, and in this case I think the upper and lower parts were glowing while the central portion was not and so looked very dark by contrast. The reason for this may become clearer when we get to Chapter 8.

It was sixteen days later but at about the same time of evening when Mrs Kathleen Penton happened to open an upstairs window to let in some air against the stuffiness of the coming night. She was astonished to see 'a shining thing going along sideways in the sky from left to right. It glided over quite slowly in front of the Warminster Downs. Porthole-type windows ran along the whole length of it.' She said it was enormous and described the colour of the 'windows' as like yellow flames in a coal fire. 'It looked much like a train carriage, only with rounded ends to it, and was gently gliding sideways in the sky,' she said.

Without knowing it, Mrs Penton was describing the classic Leviathan. She had never read *Flying Saucers Have Landed* (Leslie and Adamski, 1953), but if she had she would have seen George Adamski's photograph of the very object she had described. She would have seen its enormous bulk, together with its 'windows' which are not windows at all but patches of the craft emanating more light than other surrounding parts. These seem to be concerned with the propulsion or sustaining systems and appear only when the craft is flying along horizontally. They are not reported when a Leviathan is standing vertical, ready to fly off its scouts. Then the sheer effort of holding the giant craft as lightly as thistledown seems to often involve almost all of its surface, or at least, as in the case of the Horlocks' observation, major parts of it. We are going to see that UFOs emit light from their surfaces as a spin-off from their necessary propulsion and hovering systems. This light may not be under their control; however, when they want to, they can emit light in beams like searchlights

Fig. 2.2 The author's interpretation of the probable Leviathan that Mr and Mrs Horlock saw at Warminster, Wiltshire, in June 1965.

or laser rays. There is evidence that they may even manipulate their 'natural' light aura to confuse the astounded observer.

Adamski was able to get pictures of a Leviathan because he had the right equipment – a 6-in telescope with a relatively wide field of view fitted with a camera – and he spent a great deal of his time probing the heavens for UFOs. At the time Adamski had to suffer the utmost ridicule (as he did later) and his pictures were made out to be fakes. If they were fakes, then Adamski knew very intimately what he was faking, for the dark, cigar-shaped object with the blunt ends and the 'windows' down the side has obviously been seen and described many, many times.

On a cold January night in Vista, California, over a hundred witnesses saw a brightly lit object which hovered almost directly overhead. To most observers, all that could be seen was a light, but a retired general contractor, P. K. Rothermel, who trained his 40x telescope on it was able to see that the light was on the central part of a cigar-shaped object. He estimated it to be between 8 and 10 miles high.

After hovering over Vista for some time, the object moved off towards San Diego, after which it stopped again. This time Rothermel detected lighted objects springing from the end of the big craft and circling it. There appeared to be ten or twelve, and they were paired. After they had circled the Leviathan, they took off in many directions, whereupon the mother ship left at great speed, heading southwards and upwards into the heavens and disappearing from view in moments. Another competent witness estimated that the object was about 300 ft long, which is the correct length for the kind of Leviathan we are describing here (*LUFORO*, 1962b).

If you can be mistaken about Leviathans when you are looking at them miles up, no such mistakes can be made by aircrew when these great ships take up formation with them.

Two DC3 pilots of Eastern Airlines, Clarence Chiles and John Whitted, both veterans of World War 2, had an encounter with a Leviathan very early on in the modern phase of UFO visitations. It was 23 July 1948 and they were flying their DC3 on a routine flight near Montgomery, Alabama. They described the craft as a large 'aerial submarine' and it came and circled their plane. It was about as long as a B29. The B29 Superfortress was 99 ft long, so this device was rather smaller than the classic Leviathan. However, just as in other reports of Leviathans, it glowed all over with an intense dark-blue light that quivered across the skin like the discharge in a lighting tube. There was also a double row of what they described as ports or vents along the side, from which an unearthly white light emanated (compare Fig. 2.1). Having joined formation with them for a short time, the Leviathan let out a sheet of 'flame' 50 ft long, turned upwards at an upright angle and shot off at what they estimated was a speed approaching 1,000 m.p.h. The manoeuvre so disturbed the local atmosphere that it rocked the DC3 in the blast. Aimé Michel (1957) lists a series of Leviathan observations answering to the same description by other aircrew over a wide area of the USA in the years between 1948 and 1951 – just a few of the many.

Neither Chiles nor Whitted was born when a World War 1 pilot, Flight Sub-Lieutenant J. E. Morgan, gave one of the first authentic reports of a Leviathan which he encountered on 31 January 1916 over Rochford near Southend in Essex. Morgan went up at about 8.45 p.m. in an attempt to intercept German

Zeppelins and had got to 5,000 ft or so when he became aware that there was, a little above his own level and slightly ahead to starboard, what he described as 'a sort of phantom airship with a row of what appeared to be lighted windows which looked something like a railway carriage with the blinds drawn'.

Thinking that he had sighted a hostile airship, Morgan let fly at the object, which was only about 100 ft from him, with his Webley-Scott pistol. Whereupon, he said, 'the lights alongside rose rapidly and disappeared'. In the light of what we now know about these great craft from elsewhere, Morgan's encounter was rather a David and Goliath affair, but it is also pretty clear that they would not have bothered with a stick-and-string biplane whose pilot was bravely prepared to fire his puny gun at one of the most powerful of extraterrestrial spacecraft.

Even earlier is the statement from a lady who lived in Hiram, Ohio, and was twelve years old at the time of her experience (Lorentzen, 1966). On 17 March 1903, she was called out of the house to look at what she described as 'a sausage balloon with two rows of windows on its side'. She estimated that it was a mere 200 ft up and was hanging 'motionless and level' in the southern sky. The observation lasted sufficient time for the girl's father to measure the craft's relative dimensions and find that it was maybe four times as long as it was thick, but she thought it might have been longer because it was not exactly perpendicular to their line of sight.

She said there was a light inside the end towards them that 'illuminated the inside of the ship like a kerosene lamp in a large room'. However, there seemed to be no source for this light. She described the apparent square framework under what to her was a thin covering as light appeared to come through it. The windows were placed 'equidistant from each other and in two lines of four each above and below the medial section. There were no appendages above or below the ship and no sign of life and no noises.' Eventually the great craft moved away, slowly at first and then it 'rushed out of sight at great speed'.

Here we have another form of Leviathan that looks like a dirigible. It has open ends from which a strange light emanates. It has rows of 'windows' but, unlike today, as there were no predatory aeroplanes to disturb it, it was able to come very low.

We could go on with this catalogue *ad infinitum*, but enough has been said to establish Leviathan as an incontrovertible fact. There are many other UFO shapes reported, most variations on the disc-shaped devices that have given their name to the phenomenon of 'flying saucers'. Whether there are in fact so many varieties is open to debate and we will throw some light on this in later chapters, but in this chapter we have established that Leviathan is a 'flying-saucer carrier'. It has large, open ends and is usually about 300 ft long. It is often seen with patches of light on its sides when it is in a horizontal position, with wraiths of mist-like substance wafting round it when vertical or when manoeuvring into that position. It is capable of immense acceleration and phenomenal speeds. Some parts of it may be illuminated while others are in darkness, and sometimes separate lights seen may be not individual UFOs but lighted points on a much vaster craft, the rest of whose bulk cannot be detected.

All sorts of people have seen Leviathans cruising our airspace and have never reported the fact for fear of ridicule. A good example is a lady who was once a postwoman in the Essex village where I live. It was not until I wrote an article for a local paper that she confided to me how, early one morning, she had been the only person to see a 'silver-grey airship' fly across the village very high up. She had never spoken about it to anyone before, yet she had seen a truly wonderful sight that had obviously impressed her deeply. I know how she felt, because I also have been privileged to see this same great craft and realize that I was being granted the honour of seeing advanced technology from somewhere else in the universe.

CHAPTER 3

Leviathans over Essex

NOTHING CONVINCES PEOPLE that there really are UFOs better than a personal sighting. Even those of us who were sure, because of the sheer volume of sightings, of the reality of the cigars and saucers felt much happier, and somewhat relieved, when we had what was for us an unequivocal personal sighting.

I saw my first saucer over the ancient little church at East Mersea on Mersea Island, which lies at the confluence of the Colne and Blackwater rivers south of Colchester in Essex. I had been married only a little while and we were living in a couple of rooms in a quaint sixteenth-century house on this same island, in the shadow of the big tumulus that is called Mersea Barrow.

It was a clear autumn morning and we were just walking up the path to the church door when I happened to spot a small disc high up on a line of sight right over the church roof. It was a very insubstantial sighting of a kind that must have occurred thousands of times to vast numbers of people across the world: one that is not really worth reporting but adds to the sum total of evidence for the phenomenon.

The events of 30 June 1961 were different. This was a beautiful summer's evening and we had just come back from giving our new baby daughter her first outing to Clacton. Our garage lies on the eastern side of our detached house and is somewhat set back. I was just driving in when my wife, Joyce, urgently exclaimed, 'Reverse the car!' I knew this was a command I could not ignore, so I immediately did as she asked and there, where she had just seen them, were two intensely bright lights hanging in the western sky.

We watched those lights for a few moments before Joyce remembered the baby and took her indoors. I stayed out to look

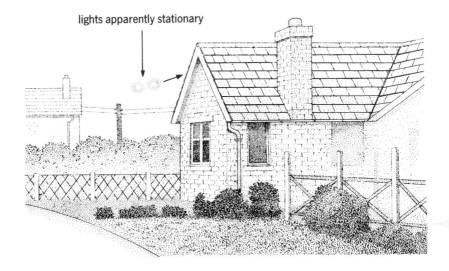

lights apparently stationary

Fig. 3.1 A sketch the author made for screening on Anglia TV, showing where the twin lights hung in the sky to the west of his house.

(Fig. 3.1). The lights were low in the sky and I had, at that time, no idea of how far away they might be. By any stretch of the imagination, they were odd. Occasionally they would fade out and then reappear. I now believe that they were small UFOs being evolved by the big one, but at the time it seemed just as though a car had been suspended in the sky with its headlights on main beam.

It was not many minutes before the lights went out, and I could just detect a blue-grey cigar-shaped object moving away northwards from where they had been (Fig. 3.2). It was soon lost behind the next-door bungalow. I dashed indoors and upstairs to our west-facing bedroom window to keep an eye on the fast-disappearing form, at the same time calling to Joyce to come up and look.

Afterwards we reconstructed this phase of the events and found that between the object moving and her arrival in the bedroom about half a minute had elapsed. This proved to be a critical time, because she had just caught the last glimpse of the object as it travelled in a climbing arc up into the north-western sky. We were able to use that time and our positions later to prove

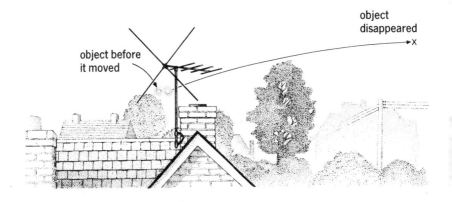

Fig. 3.2 A sketch to show the view from an upstairs west-facing window that allowed the speed of the Leviathan to be calculated.

that this object was finally moving at a speed that was quite out of this world – about 2,500 m.p.h. to be exact.

However, at the time I did not know that. Although it was apparently so far away, I was convinced that what had been the origin of the lights and had then moved away so rapidly was a Leviathan, but I needed more proof. So I wrote to the local Colchester newspaper, the *Essex County Standard*, and they published my account. In response to my plea for witnesses to come forward, I had up to a dozen letters and an almost equal number of phone calls.

As an active member of a UFO research organization, I knew what I had to do. So the next few days saw me interviewing as many of these witnesses as possible to see if their accounts tallied.

To cut a long story short, I found, after much extra correspondence and several interviews, that there were two schools of thought: first, those who were convinced that the object and its lights were an aeroplane, and second, those who thought 'flying saucer' when they saw either the lights or the object or both. Undoubtedly, some people did see an aeroplane in the area of the stationary object, but there were enough other observations to make it quite evident that our object was not an aeroplane.

In the course of my investigations I had a few strokes of luck. Being a physics lecturer at the local technical college brought me into contact with several scientifically minded students who had seen the object. For one thing, there had been a disco at the college that evening and, as it had been warm, many students had spilled out into the open. Some of them were able to stand exactly where they had stood that Friday evening and pinpoint the direction of the lights against the building. A compass told me that, as the college lay on the line between my home and the object, we had indeed been looking at the same thing.

Having been scientifically trained, I never quite believe anything that cannot be corroborated independently by at least two witnesses. It is much more satisfactory with UFO sightings to have more than two, but the nature of the phenomenon is such that if you get two independent reports that tally you are lucky.

In the event, I got three on the line of sight, because another student who was at home, half-way between my house and the object, was also able to confirm the direction. He gave me an independent check on the length too by visualizing this on a ruler held at arm's length. His estimate was twice my own, made in the same way, and so, as he was twice as near as I was, this confirmed the length.

In the same sort of way, witnesses agreed with what I thought the thing looked like. They supported my description of the blue-grey colour, the apparent length and the direction in which it moved, and above all they gave me its position. I got witnesses from places all round the object and, when I drew their lines of sight on a map, I found the 'cocked hat' where they crossed was over a rural place called Forry's Green. This lies a couple of miles north-west of the small Essex town of Halstead and so was over 20 miles from us.

Those 20 miles were the distance I wanted. With that information I could scale up the apparent length and I arrived at a 300-ft-long object. It had to be a Leviathan. Also, I could now find out how fast it was travelling when we lost it – the 2,500 m.p.h. already quoted. From zero to this phenomenal speed in half a minute! Certainly a cosmic kind of acceleration.

The final witness to confirm that this was indeed Leviathan was the man who had managed to train field glasses on the object and said, without being prompted, 'It had portholes down the side.' He had been even further from Forry's Green than I had and to see the characteristic light patches at that range meant that they must have made a strong contrast with the rest of the hull.

The fact that to the naked eye it looked grey-blue against a bright summer-evening sky also meant that the whole hull must have been emanating light, otherwise it would have just looked black.

The 'aeroplane' theory could be dropped from consideration once I had calculated the likely height at which I first saw it as 13,000 ft. These 'aeroplane' enthusiasts said that what they had seen was an aircraft circling the nearby US Air Force base of Wethersfield, but no aircraft will circle an airfield at such a height.

However, the mystery was not entirely solved. You have to sift the reports people make very carefully, because they do not always tally in every respect. Soon some of mine began to show discrepancies. I did find, though, that lights were seen in various parts of Essex and Hertfordshire for the rest of the night, and this ties in well with the carrier-craft theory.

The 'saucers' that disembarked over Forry's Green went off on their various unknown missions throughout most of the hours of darkness, as testified to by witnesses from as far apart as Grays in south Essex and Ware in Hertfordshire, as well as several in the environs of Colchester and Halstead. The lights were almost universally described as 'twins', just as in the Vista sighting mentioned in Chapter 2. The most spectacular experience was had by a lady in Kelvedon, south-west of Colchester, who at 3.30 a.m. was amazed to see two hovering lights 'the size of tea plates' not far from her house, in the direction of Mersea Island.

The corroborated facts of this case meant that it got some attention from the media. First of all, I found myself at Anglia TV in Norwich, doing an interview, and subsequently Associated Rediffusion in Kingsway, London, included it in a programme they used to run called *Here and Now*. This was one of the very few national TV slots that did not set out to make us UFO buffs appear at best mistaken and at worst deranged by including a psychologist on the programme.

However, it is a poor reflection on the TV networks that they have never steeled themselves to make an in-depth documentary on the UFO scene, which is one of the greatest mysteries of our time. What has been done instead is largely aimed not at elucidating the matter, and trying to make sense of what has been experienced by so many unimpeachable witnesses, but at leaving the viewer quite sure that the witnesses are liars, hallucinators or plainly mental. It is a very sad state of affairs and shows how little objectivity there is in this vital issue.

The events of 30 June 1961 were not, however, the end of the matter. Five years later almost to the day the telephone rang a good half an hour before I was due to set off for work. It was an excited college keeper asking if I had seen the 'thing over the Hilly Fields'.

The Hilly Fields is a public open space just to the west of the technical college where I worked and so the direction indicated was just the same as it had been five years before. It was now 8 a.m. rather than 9.30 p.m., but sure enough, when I crashed the receiver down on its rest and ran outside, there in the western sky was the object.

This time I had my field glasses ready. The object was vertical, with the top end glinting and the signs of smoky wreathings of cloud wafting round its lower end. This end was varying shades of a rather indistinct darkness and it reminded me for all the world of an aerial jellyfish with filmy, waving tentacles.

I knew the information I had to have and was soon back on the phone, asking those watching to measure the angle of elevation. It is nearly 5 miles from my home to the college and with their elevation and mine it was an easy job to calculate that the device was about 9 miles high and some 15 miles west of the college. Remarkably, when I arrived there at about 8.50 a.m., I was able to measure the angle myself, as the thing was still in position and had been for the past hour and a half.

I was convinced that this was another Leviathan – maybe the same one that had visited us five years previously. On this occasion it had decided to stay for a very long time. To add to my conviction, some of the night cleaning staff saw a 'star-like object' shoot out from the position of the big one. They had better glasses than mine and one of them was able to sketch what he had seen (Fig. 3.3). The spot below the great craft was not far from where it had been before. This time no one could say that this was an aeroplane, for the total duration of the sighting was three full hours. By then the object was drifting away upwards towards the west and we tired of peering at its diminishing image.

The sketch that the cleaner made looks like a balloon, but it was easy to prove it could have been no such thing. I rang the Meteorological Office and found that winds at the object's height

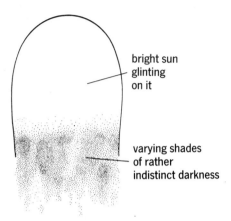

bright sun
glinting
on it

varying shades
of rather
indistinct darkness

Fig. 3.3 A rough sketch of the presumed Leviathan seen from the author's home in July 1967 using field glasses.

were from the north-west, at a speed of some 20 knots. So a balloon would have drifted 60 miles in three hours and would have been well out over the North Sea by then. Our 'balloon' not only stayed where it was but even withdrew upwards, against the direction of the wind.

The most amazing fact about this second sighting so close to the first lay in its timing. A year viewed from space is not the same as one viewed from earth and is called a tropical year. It is five hours and forty-eight minutes longer than the solar year. When I did the calculation allowing for the leap year, I was astonished to find that five exact tropical years brought us to 9 a.m., 2 July 1966 – the exact time of the second sighting. If the space denizens had wanted to rendezvous over the same spot at a time when the earth had gone round the sun exactly five times, then they were absolutely on time, while for us they were a day and a half late.

Personally I was elated at the reappearance of the Leviathan after an exact span of five years. It showed some semblance of ordered action in what is a frustratingly random and unpredictable set of phenomena.

But one coincidence does not make a theory. Those who watched the skies on the evening on 3 July 1971 – five tropical years after the second visitation – saw nothing as it was an entirely cloudy night. If Leviathan was there again, then no earth-bound watcher could see it. However, there was a third event. This occurred on the evening of 9 July 1967 – approximately a year after the last event.

An acquaintance who lived 100 yd down the road from me in the Essex village of Elmstead Market knocked on my door and excitedly asked if I had seen the object in the sky. His wife had first noticed it at about 8.15 p.m. and had been looking at it ever since. It was then 9.15 p.m. and, lo and behold, there was a light, slightly brighter than a first-magnitude star, to the south-east of us. Through his low-magnification telescope, it proved to be a vast egg-shaped object (akin to those in Figs. 3.3 and 3.4), with an apparently flabby exterior that seemed to move about almost as though the wind were blowing it. It had a yellow look, with a bright centre and a bright 'lump' underneath. The most obvious conclusion was that it was sky-hook balloon but, just as in 1966, it was easy to prove that with the upper winds prevailing, in an hour and a half a balloon would have drifted over 50 miles to the south-east and been well out of sight.

Thus we had three events in six years. The last two were very similar in appearance, but were we the only ones to see this kind of device? One morning in April 1967 a man working in a quarry on the coast of south Devon had his attention caught by a flock of squabbling seagulls. Looking up to see what the commotion was about, his attention was caught by a triangular-shaped object glistening in the sunlight and very high up. At first, just like us, he thought he was looking at a balloon, but again, just like us, it did not drift.

The Berry Head Coastguard Station was nearby and soon the officer on duty had the object fixed in his powerful binoculars. He estimated it to be at about 15,000 ft. He then telephoned six off-duty colleagues down in Brixham and they, and hundreds of others, watched the object. Not only the coastguard but the police and RAF were inundated with calls from people who saw the object (Fig. 3.4).

Just as with our Leviathan sightings, the object was in no hurry and, after an hour and ten minutes, it moved slowly north-westwards. It appeared to be rotating slowly and there was a dark patch on its side. A plane, said by witnesses to be ten times smaller than the object, then flew over it and was seen to dive and make an approach from below. What then transpired was lost to

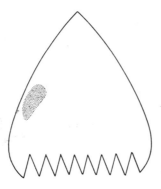

Fig 3.4   The Berry Head object, very similar to what had been seen the previous April.

view by thickening cloud, which was said by the Meteorological Office to be at 22,000 ft. According to them, winds at that altitude and above were from the north-east and no less than 40 knots in speed. Just as in our Essex sightings, if this had been a balloon, it would have drifted 50 miles to the south-west. This object was able to hold itself stationary against the wind and also to move across it.

Unbeknown to me, at that time there had been a Devon sighting of what must have been another Leviathan just eleven days earlier than ours of 30 June 1961. The sighting lasted for over an hour and the object was stationary throughout. This time the winds at its altitude were some 20 knots from the west and again there were hundreds of witnesses.

There are good reasons why a Leviathan standing on end while it releases or embarks flying saucers may be confused with a balloon. It is, after all, roughly the same shape as one of those long, flabby sky-hook balloons that used to be flown from Cardington in Bedfordshire with a payload of photographic plates to obtain scientific evidence from cosmic rays. However, such balloons are only that tall, elongated shape on the ground. As they ascend to more rarefied levels, they assume the round shape of classic balloons. The glinting, as though the thing is polished metal, we will explain in a later chapter and the waving, shimmering, cloudy effect that surrounds some, if not all, parts has been seen in the French sighting described in Chapter 2. Dark patches or portions appear both on the base and elsewhere on Leviathans and other UFOs, while the slow revolution sometimes seen may not be the craft itself rotating but only its cloudy exterior.

If today you should see one of these great spacecraft and be told that it is a balloon, you can often quite easily prove that it is nothing of the sort. In any case, balloons as big as a Leviathan have never been flown and at the present time no one is flying sky-hook balloons. Leviathans now operate at extreme altitude and at such altitudes a balloon would be much more nearly spherical. It would not, therefore, be the same shape as a cloudy, wavy, cigar-shaped Leviathan.

CHAPTER
4

Grappling with George Adamski

FOR THOSE OF US who aspired to being ufologists in the early days, one of the biggest problems we had to contend with was the testimony of George Adamski.

'I am George Adamski, philosopher, student, teacher, saucer researcher. My home is Palomar Gardens on the southern slopes of Mount Palomar, California.' Thus starts Book Two of *Flying Saucers Have Landed* (Leslie and Adamski, 1953), which has been in print continuously since its first publication.

Before he gets down to the serious business of the contact he made with a UFOnaut, Adamski describes his telescopes and how he initially became aware of the presence of alien spacecraft in our atmosphere. He saw his first Leviathan in 1946, describing it as 'similar in shape to a giant dirigible and apparently motionless'. Later he says, 'While we were still watching, it pointed its nose upwards and quickly shot up into the sky, leaving a fiery trail behind it which remained visible for a good five minutes.' Hundreds of people saw this event and the San Diego radio carried a story about it.

He then goes on to describe his own part in the rising tide of interest in the subject of flying saucers, so many of which were being seen in America at that time. He took photographs with his highly mobile 6-in reflector telescope and sent them, on request, to a local naval electronics laboratory. He never saw them again and the laboratory denied ever having received them. Adamski's first brush with the authorities led him to observe more diligently than before but to keep his own counsel. He had some success when he attempted to obtain good pictures of UFOs, but it took a great deal of his time over several years. Without bitterness, he tells how he was accused of commercialism and deception when, in an attempt to recoup some of his inevitable losses, he tried to market his pictures.

The persistence with which George Adamski sought his quarry was twisted in some quarters into an argument against him. If you go out looking for flying saucers, ran the argument, then you are bound to end up seeing them. To which the logical answer is, if you never look for something, how can you ever expect to find it?

The photographs that Adamski took of Leviathans in March 1951 and May 1952 are, I believe, genuine and some of the best ever taken. One of them, reproduced in *Flying Saucers Have Landed*, shows the classic blunt-ended cigar shape surrounded by discs of light. The whole series (only the last of four was reproduced) showed a gradually increasing number of discs as the large craft 'evolved' them. This Leviathan does not reveal the luminous patches, but another picture does (Fig. 4.1), proving that Adamski was photographing a true Leviathan. He also took close-up and detailed pictures of a type of disc-shaped UFO which has become known as Adamski's saucer (see Fig. 4.4).

The evidence of Adamski's pictures has been corrobated by a photograph taken by an unimpeachable witness which can be shown to be the same kind of craft. I believe that the arguments in favour of Adamski's saucer are sufficiently strong for us to treat the photographs reproduced in *Flying Saucers Have Landed* as genuine.

It is when you become convinced that a man who has been held up to so much ridicule by so many over such a long period is genuine that your problem begins. Not only did Adamski describe how he took the pictures that logic says are genuine; he also described in detail his meeting with a man from a disc-shaped craft that landed near him in the Californian desert, where he went with a party of friends because he had a 'feeling' that he might possibly meet such an entity there.

He says that he did meet this person – a man of normal human proportions whose only possibly odd attribute was that he was surprisingly beautiful in the classical Greek tradition – and they conversed by means of telepathy.

Fig 4.1 A sketch of the Leviathan that George Adamski photographed in May 1952, showing the classic 'cigar' shape and the bright patches so often described as 'ports' or 'windows'.

That they made such communication is certainly not beyond the bounds of possibility. Telepathy is now recognized as a scientific fact and governments have spent great sums of money trying to use it as a form of unjammable radio link between soldiers on the field of battle, as well as for other purposes. In Uri Geller's *My Story* (1975) there are reproductions of some of his telepathic responses to drawings made under rigorous test conditions and, amazingly, published in the ultra-conventional scientific magazine *Nature*. The shapes that Geller has picked up are in some cases almost identical, while in others they relate to the ideas expressed in the original target drawings. The ability of UFOnauts to take mental control of people they wish to examine or maybe 'electronically tag' has been reported sufficiently often and in enough detail for it to be recognized as a fact. These visitors from elsewhere are in many cases very advanced in methods of psychological control and therefore would be equally so in telepathy.

In any case, they obviously knew that Adamski was a safe contactee and this meeting was set up by them. They subjected him, a microscopic speck on the surface of the earth, to surveillance, as they have many others, and his 'feeling' was undoubtedly a telepathic instruction to be at a certain place at a certain time to make the rendezvous. However, what is intriguing is the form of surveillance by which a particular human being could be known to be the person most fitted to attempt the meeting – one of five who drove into the desert on the 20 November 1952. To me the significant point is not that Adamski made the contact – I believe the evidence suggests that he did – but how these space denizens managed to monitor him, and how many more of us are being monitored without our ever being aware of it?

However, there are other curious mysteries to be probed. One concerns the film-holders that Adamski used in the camera of the telescope he took along to the hoped-for meeting. Having nothing else, Adamski gave one to the spaceman as a parting gift, and the latter took it with him when he flew off.

Less than a month later, on 13 December, this film-holder was returned to Adamski by either the same or a similar saucer, of which he was able to get fine, detailed photographs. These are the pictures that appeared in *Flying Saucers Have Landed* and gave us our first real detailed look at the classic 'flying saucer'.

If evidence is required of human-like intelligence acting behind the UFO phenomenon, then reasonable proof of the return of this film-holder would help to establish it. For the film-holder, when returned, had had the original photograph removed and in its place was what proved to be some form of writing, plus a drawing of an eye-shaped device (Fig. 4.2). The writing has never, to my knowledge, been adequately deciphered, and while it has resemblances to certain ancient scripts, particularly Phoenician, only a few of the 'letters' resemble any known language. Obviously, the first conclusion is that George Adamski fabricated the device and the writing to back up his story of a return visit of the saucer. However, there is more to it than that.

In 1963 Marcel Homet, an explorer and archaeologist with over a dozen books to his credit and at one time Professor of Classical Arabic at the University of Algiers, published a book about his explorations in Amazonia, *Sons of the Sun* (1963). It describes, among other things, his work at the Pedra Pintada, or Painted Rock, near Tarame in Brazil. This rock resembles a vast boulder cast down upon the plain on which it lies, but it is 300 ft long, nearly as wide and almost 100 ft high. It is covered with inscriptions and has an immense representation of a snake painted on it whose mouth is the entrance to a cave in the rock. Homet considers it is related to the 'Cosmic Egg' theme of Mediterranean and Celtic cultures. In fact, his book is directed towards showing the remarkable similarities between the cultures revealed by the inscriptions, dolmens etc. that are found in Amazonia and those of Celtic and Mediterranean lands. However, at the back of *Sons of the Sun*, Homet gives a set of inscriptions that he says he found during his expedition, together with an almost exact replica of the eye-shaped device that appeared on Adamski's film-holder (Fig. 4.3).

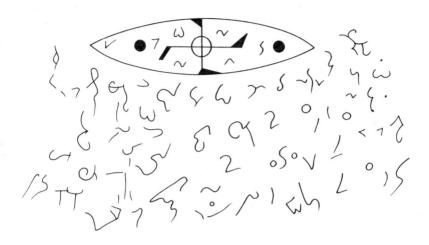

Fig 4.2   The majority of the symbols and the stylized 'saucer' device which appeared on the photographic plate that was returned to Adamski on 13 December 1952. The cross-section shows considerable similarities to a 'vaid' (see Fig. 16.5).

Fig. 4.3   The symbols and 'vaid' drawing which were given by Marcel Homet in his *Sons of the Sun*. Several of the glyphs are identical to those in Fig. 4.2, but the 'writing' in the vaid device is different.

At first sight, the sceptic would say that Homet 'borrowed' Adamski's glyphs to add more mystery to his book, but this does not really add up. What did Homet, a well-known explorer and archaeologist in his own right, have to gain from such a move? In a letter to a UFO researcher, Miss Rey d'Aquila, sent from São Paulo on 7 September 1961, he concludes:

> With regard to the oval design, which I have published in *Sons of the Sun*, I have discovered same in the neighbourhood of the Pedra Pintada (Painted Rock), Amazonia. The other 'graffiti' surrounding the oval have also been discovered by me in the same area, but they have been very much effaced through the effect of time (which fact, by the way, denotes an age of about 12,000 to 14,000 years BC), so much so that, if I had not seen them later in the book *Flying Saucers Have Landed*, published by Adamski, I would not have paid any particular attention to them.

Homet was also interviewed for the *International Paranormal Bulletin* (April 1962), run by a group of ufologists in Amsterdam. In this journal, Homet says:

> The history of the inscriptions is a very remarkable one. I read the book by Adamski and I was surprised to find the same signs, however not in the same order. Only the oval drawn by me is totally identical with the one of Adamski's. The other signs I have found during my expeditions in separate places. I only brought them together with the oval shape to prove that one can find these similar signs everywhere in the Amazon territory. Therefore I never took the trouble to decipher them.

Thus we have an enigma. Adamski assumes that his signs are 'writing from another planet', while Homet discovers them on this one. Maybe they are both. It seems perfectly feasible to me, seeing that the scope for UFO visitations to this planet stretches back to an unknown antiquity, for the signs in Amazonia to be part of a language which is still known to the UFO denizens after a span of say 15,000 or so years, and maybe they expected this intriguing tie-up to occur – maybe caused it to occur – so that the glyphs in Adamski's film-holder should be corroborated.

We can find another drawing similar to the oval one in a book by Robert Charroux called *The Mysterious Unknown* (1972). Here the device is said to be a drawing of an inter-stellar spacecraft called a 'vaidorge', but Charroux's source was entirely different from either Adamski's or Homet's. We will examine this and another source of the same lens-shaped device in Chapter 16. This source will also reveal glyphs similar to, but only in a few cases the same as, those published by Adamski and Homet.

Adamski's saucer became a believable reality to me when it was corroborated by Leonard Cramp in his book *Space, Gravity and the Flying Saucer* (1954). Cramp, an aeronautical engineer and draughtsman who at one time worked for the Saunders-Roe aircraft company on the Isle of Wight, had obviously seen Adamski's pictures but had also obtained a copy of a similar picture taken by a thirteen-year-old schoolboy, Stephen Darbishire, on 15 February 1954. Stephen was the son of a doctor who lived at Coniston in Lancashire, and on this particular morning a certain restless feeling sent him and his eight-year-old cousin Adrian Myer off up the steep hill that lay between his home and Coniston Water. He took with him his simple Kodak camera, as he hoped to get some photographs of birds, bird-watching being his great hobby.

It was a cold day, with broken cloud at low levels but enough humidity for the top of the 2,575 ft-high Coniston Old Man to be lost in cloud. Adrian saw the saucer first, but both boys saw it descend and disappear behind some rising ground, and just before it was lost to view Stephen managed to take a photo of it. It was lost to view for only a few seconds before it shot up into the sky and disappeared into cloud with what was described as a 'deep, swishing sound', in contrast to its previous total silence.

Stephen said it had a silvery, glassy appearance but, by the way he described it, he thought it was translucent:

> It was a solid metal-like thing, with a dome, portholes, and three bumps or landing domes underneath. In the centre the underneath was darker and pointed like a cone. At first three portholes were visible, but then it turned slightly and we saw four.

Cramp personally investigated this important event, staying with the Darbishires as their guest and re-enacting the whole

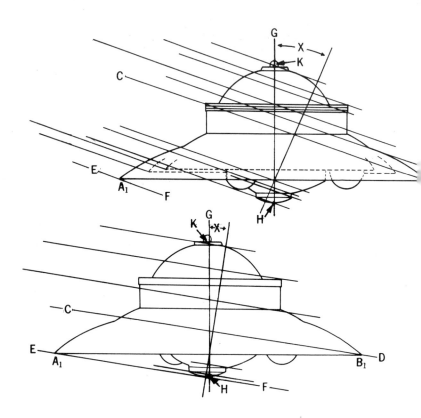

Fig. 4.4 The orthographic projections by which Leonard Cramp showed (in *Space, Gravity and the Flying Saucer*) that the fuzzy Darbishire photograph was identical in proportions to the much clearer Adamski picture. See also Photo 15.

episode. He, like Stephen's father and many other people, became quite convinced that the boys had seen an Adamski-type saucer. One fact stands out in Cramp's investigation and it concerns the portholes. Stephen had never seen *Flying Saucers Have Landed*, but he had seen one of the Adamski photographs when it appeared in *Illustrated* on 30 September 1953. However, that picture, like all those in *Flying Saucers Have Landed*, showed only three ports. Stephen Darbishire was adamant that he and his cousin had seen four. It appears that unpublished pictures of Adamski's saucer also show four ports in a row, but in the book the fourth was either not visible or had been trimmed off before reproduction.

'Maybe,' said Stephen, 'ours was another type.' Not at all. What Stephen had seen was an identical device to the one

Adamski had photographed and, using orthographic projection, Leonard Cramp showed that they projected into the same device (Photo 15). In his book, Cramp makes some play on the fact that although Stephen was quite certain that he had set his camera on infinity, the picture of the saucer was blurred and therefore out of focus. That need not be an argument, as we shall see in later chapters, for the radiation aura of the saucer can emit invisible rays to which the film is sensitive but not the eye. Thus while, to the boys, the visible light from the saucer gave it a distinct appearance, the photographic emulsion could have picked up the aura, so rendering the outline fuzzy. This may also be the reason that many UFO pictures are equally fuzzy.

So Adamski's saucer had appeared again and there was photographic evidence for it. This convinced many of us who were trying to bring some scientific reasoning to bear on the saucer problem that here we had a real object with real dimensions. Maybe, therefore, we could do some work on this one device and perhaps draw solid facts from the welter of rumour and speculation that surrounded the saucer phenomenon at that time – and has, incidentally, done so ever since.

CHAPTER

5

Progress towards Propulsion

THE 1950s AND 1960s were heady days for those of us who were scientifically trained and had an interest in flying saucers. A great amount of hard evidence was coming our way and it included some from rather bizarre events. In 1962–4 we were studying, as best we could, bits of the most intriguing item I have ever had the luck to handle. This was the so-called Silpho Moor object.

One evening in 1958 a 'space toy' landed in a field near the tiny hamlet of Silpho in Yorkshire. Silpho Moor lies about 5 miles north-west of Scarborough and in the shadow of the giant domes of the Fylingdales early warning radar complex. The copper shell of the Silpho Moor object was glowing hot when it landed, but it was not burned up, as it would have been had it fallen from space. The shell was a classic saucer shape, except that its cross-section was the shape of the vaidorge shown on page 00, being equally curved on top and bottom surfaces. It had much the same shape as a flattened version of a metal bed-warmer in which you put a 60-watt bulb. There was a circular opening in the top and inside was some copper piping and a copper scroll with writing on it. I did not take much interest in the scroll at the time, but I handled parts of the shell, because we wanted to get expert opinions about its metallurgy and its amazingly complex construction.

The British Non-Ferrous Metals Research Association reported that the copper of the shell was of exceptional purity. This immediately put it out of the normal run of coppers that a hoaxer could have obtained. Commercially available coppers have different impurity atoms added to make them tougher, or easier to cut, more suitable for the electronics industry, etc. The purity of the Silpho Moor copper showed that it was not an off-the-shelf material from a supplier of industrial metals.

The copper scroll material was analysed by the Department of Metallurgy at Manchester University and they came up with a similar degree of purity. However, the scroll was not a single sheet, but consisted of three very thin sheets laminated together. Again, what hoaxer would have added such a refinement, even if he or she could have worked the material in the first place?

Then there was the 'solder' which formed the conical tip of the object. Both the Cavendish Laboratory at Cambridge and Manchester University came to the same conclusion: it was a metal resembling lead. But this did not mean that it *was* lead. Solder-like material falling from a UFO has been well documented in a Brazilian incident – the so-called 'Campinas sighting' (Maney, 1962).

On 23 December 1954, several UFOs were sighted over Campinas and one, flying low, was seen to drop a silvery liquid material which fell to the ground as hot molten metal. The material was collected by Professor B. G. Nascimento, who submitted it to the Young Laboratories for analysis. Their chief chemist, Dr V. Maffei, reported that the sample was 88.91 per cent tin and 11.09 per cent oxygen. The latter was simply the result of oxidization as the metal cooled and absolutely no other element was found; this was, in fact, 100 per cent tin. There were a number of other lumps of metal found in the vicinity and some were submitted to Professor N. Meltz, who reported that they were antimony-free solder containing various proportions of lead and tin. The results were corroborated by two other scientific laboratories, and so lead and tin, looking like solder, have actually been seen to fall from UFOs.

We became convinced that our 'space toy' was no ordinary hoax object when we discovered that the copper sheets of the shell had a most curious structure. The research chemist of our group, George Elliot, was unable to show any signs of crystalline structure or of normal means of fabrication. It was as if the copper were formed as one giant single crystal – something unknown in the world of metallurgy, but possibly something that was necessary if the metal were to act as a superconductor.

However, it was the construction of the inverted saucer-shaped top surface that really excited me. It showed beyond doubt that the object was not a hoax. On examination the shell proved to be formed from a sandwich of copper sheets with a material looking rather like the adhesive Araldite as the filling. But even that was not simple, for it was found to be a form of polystyrene of such high molecular weight that Elliot was sure no one had managed to produce anything like it commercially and was doubtful if it had even been fabricated in the laboratory. To add an important piece to the puzzle, it had a magnetic powder dispersed through it. I am going to call this construction a 'magnite sandwich' for want of a better name. The copper sheet on the top of the sandwich was thicker than that on the underside, and this set me thinking. If this really were a toy flying saucer, then could this magnite-sandwich construction be a small-scale version of what was used on the big ones? I had seen something like it before, because for some reason Leonard Cramp, when he drew an 'engineers'' view of Adamski's saucer (Fig. 5.1), showed one side of the cupola with a double skin. However, he did not go as far as to continue this into what we will call the 'bell surface' of the saucer. That double skin and the Silpho Moor object's magnite sandwich pointed to the idea of a circuit, and so to an electric current flowing in the surfaces.

A major contribution to the realization that no one could have hoaxed the Silpho Moor object was the complex structure of the outer edges of its bell-shaped surface, where the thick and thin copper sheets met. We found that there was a minutely thin sheet of something resembling wood between the top and bottom copper sheets, where they met at the rim. So they were not joined but separated by an insulator.

I took the fragment I had to the chief scientist of a research complex near my home and, not telling him the origin of the specimen, asked if he'd ever seen anything like it before. Obviously he had not, but he did a few tests, one of which was to find out the electrical resistance between the upper and lower layers of the magnite sandwich through the rim, where it appeared they were joined. This proved that they were indeed separated by a very thin electrically resistive layer which was not evident to the eye. So the two layers were not in actual contact but given enough voltage, electric current could flow from top to bottom – or vice versa.

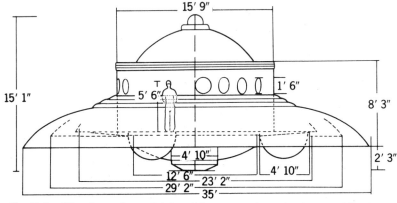

Fig. 5.1 The dimensions of Adamski's saucer show that humanoids of normal proportions could act as crew (from Leonard Cramp's *Space, Gravity and the Flying Saucer*).

The Electromagnetic (EM) Effect

By this time it was evident that many UFOs had, either by design or accident, a very strong electromagnetic field about them and, when they were close to vehicles, could interfere with ignition systems. That it was interference with the high-tension side of the ignition was made evident by reports like the following. On 14 November 1954, near Forli in Italy, a luminous red UFO had flown over two tractors being driven along a road side by side. One of them was petrol-driven and the other diesel. The engine of the petrol tractor died as soon as the UFO came near, while that of the diesel kept going (Lorentzen, 1966).

It is not possible to tell whether all UFOs have this ability, or even whether it is just a pure accident arising from their propulsion system, but the number of so-called EM cases is legion and sometimes a special kind of UFO seems to be involved. For instance, there is a report of trucks and cars on highways around Levelland, Texas, being stopped and their lights doused by what were mainly described as 'neon eggs' (Vallée, 1966). They were big eggs, estimated to be 150–200 ft long and of various hues. However, the descriptions from a substantial number of witnesses made it evident that the incidents were all due to the same or similar objects.

It was just before midnight on 2 November 1957 and the first report came from Pedro Saucedo and José Salav. Their truck was 'beaten up' by a low-flying UFO which came straight across them with, as Saucedo said, 'a great sound and a rush of wind. It sounded like thunder and the truck rocked from blast. I felt a lot of heat.' As the object approached their lights went out and the motor died, but as soon as it had gone the truck started normally. An hour later Jim Wheeler, who was driving his car 4 miles east of Levelland, had a similar experience, due to 'a blazing 200-ft-long egg-shaped object' sitting on the road ahead of him. Again he lost his lights and his engine.

This report was followed not long afterwards by another from José Alvarez, who was some 10 miles north-north-east of Levelland and reported that he had also lost his lights and engine when he drove near a 'bright egg-shaped object on the road'. At 1.15 a.m. James Long had been driving along a farm road 5 miles north-west of Levelland when he also encountered a 200-ft-long egg-shaped mass that glowed 'like a neon sign'. Again his engine and lights failed when the object was less than a matter of 100 yd away. There were several incidents of a similar nature in the area at the same time.

The chronology of events indicates that they could all have been occasioned by the same craft and there is nothing to suggest that this 'neon egg' was not just playing games with the vehicles around Levelland on this particular night – maybe testing its ability to halt vehicles in their tracks or maybe just ensuring that they did not get too close. When you are dealing with an intelligently controlled set of objects, then it is often impossible to decide exactly what their motives might be.

The Wildman Case

It was not these events but one nearer home that first gave me some clues as to the magnitude of the EM effect coming from UFOs.

Ronald Wildman was a car-delivery driver. One frosty February morning in 1962, he set off from his home in Luton to deliver a Vauxhall Victor car to Swansea. He started early and the trees and verges were sparkling with hoar frost as he drove down the Ivinghoe–Tring road at 3.30 a.m. (Fig. 5.2).

On rounding a bend he was startled by and 'almost ran into' a big disc-shaped flying object which was hovering over the road. He described the UFO as 30–40 ft across, with a curved or domed upper surface and a straight lower edge. There were eight to ten dark, squarish portholes or vents equally spaced across and just above the lower rim. He came as close as 20 ft, but could not get any closer even if he had wanted to, for the saucer moved off down the road at about 20 m.p.h., with the car 'in tow'. At least it seemed like that to Wildman, whose engine nearly stalled at his nearest approach to the object, forcing him to change down rapidly to a lower gear. They travelled some 50 yd of the road this way and then the UFO had to pass over the roadside trees, and the hoar frost from them was showered on to the roof of the car 'like rain or hail'. Immediately a ring of vapour appeared around the periphery of the object and just below it. The UFO then accelerated upwards and away to the right at a fantastic speed and disappeared from view. The car

Fig. 5.2   Artist's impression of the encounter between Ronald Wildman and the saucer near Ivinghoe, Buckinghamshire.

suddenly responded quite normally and a somewhat shaken driver went first to the Aylesbury police to report what he had seen and then on his way without further incident.

Wildman said that the trees swayed and writhed about when the saucer was near, and this motion has been reported on other occasions when UFOs are close to trees. I personally do not believe that it has anything to do with wind. Rather it may be connected to the way crops are laid by UFO activity in the now well-known crop-circle phenomenon. The EM emanations from the craft somehow interact with the essential fluids flowing in the branches, etc., resulting in a situation like that experienced by the armature of an electric motor in the latter's magnetic field coils.

An Important Experiment

In the Wildman case, because of the way the saucer acted on the trees, the distance between saucer and car could be estimated with some accuracy. So here was a chance to answer, in part at least, the important question, what order of magnetism would the saucer need to stop a car?

This and other believable reports made me very keen to find out if magnetism could stop a car. Luckily I had the facilities to do an experiment on my own vehicle; first by winding a coil (a solenoid) on a cylindrical former large enough to accommodate the ignition coil of my Ford Cortina (Fig. 5.3).

Because I was teaching physics at a technical college, I was able to inveigle the motor-vehicles shop into allowing me to connect up my solenoid with the coil inside it to their heavy-current set-up while still keeping it connected to the car (Watts, 1964).

We ran the engine at high revs, progressively increasing the current, and so the magnetism, in the solenoid. I was disappointed to find that despite giving it all the amps we had, nothing much happened. Then I had an idea. We were using DC. What happened if we changed to AC?

The result was dramatic. With less current than before, the engine slowed down very considerably. If we had had more current available, I think we would have stopped the engine dead, and of course we had only one frequency – 50 hertz (cycles per second).

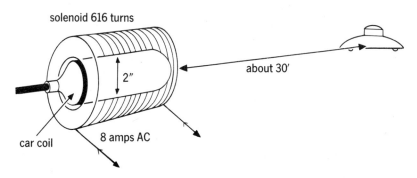

Fig. 5.3   The solenoid the author wound to surround the coil of his car which showed the kind of magnetism that could interfere with the ignition.

Maybe some other frequency would have been more effective.

What had happened was that the core of the coil had become saturated with magnetism so that it could respond only partially to the changes in current. This weakened the spark at the plugs and so the engine lost power. This in turn made me realize that the magnetism surrounding saucers was probably alternating, which prompted the question, why? It was a question that would have to wait for important ideas that were also forming at the time.

As a scientifically trained person, I have never liked things that look technical to be incomprehensible. Strange they may be, but we are getting to the stage in science today when what the saucers are able to do may not be too many decades into the future for us to emulate. It will be a slow dawning of understanding, stemming from small beginnings, and it may need the new Einstein everyone is waiting for to give the insight, but I think we may well do it in the next century. That may be one of the reasons for the intense interest UFOnauts are taking in us today – vastly more than at any time in the recorded past. They know at present that we can hop off this planet only with a vast expenditure of brute force, but say we learned their more subtle ways? Then going into space would be not just for highly trained astronauts and a much wider spectrum of humanity could find its way into the domains that the UFOs have had all to themselves for who knows how long. I suppose, to adopt a sci-fi term, we would then be made to join the 'Federation' of space races and sign the 'Space Convention', restricting us to obey the laws of minimum-intervention, as the UFOnauts appear to do.

Towards a Flying Carpet

With the help of all these clues, and others I have not mentioned, I was beginning to get an idea of how a surface like the bell surface of a saucer could lift itself. I thought of the ancient Persian ideas of 'flying carpets'. Maybe they were not so far-fetched; perhaps in an earlier civilization people had flown on surfaces that lifted themselves without visible means of support. But for me it all had to be in line with Newton and Einstein, as well as Clerk Maxwell, who formulated the basis of the electromagnetic theory.

The ignition-coil experiment had shown me the level of magnetic field that would have to remain at a car for the car to be 'controlled' by the saucer. I was now able to work back and find the size of the field at the saucer itself. When I did this, I came up with a figure that was large but not impossibly so. It was the kind of field strength that our own scientific research groups are working towards, using special techniques.

The unit that gives the strength of a magnetic field is the tesla, named after the Croatian electrical pioneer Nikola Tesla, who spent his later life in the United States and who died in 1943 at the age of eighty-seven. Interestingly enough, it was he who first developed means of using alternating current, but he is maybe best remembered for the Tesla coil, a device which was the father of the coils used on cars to generate the spark. Incidentally, Tesla and Marconi both picked up radio signals of unknown origin in the very earliest days of radio. They were first detected in 1901, but were still being received as late as 1924 and consisted of the dot-dot-dot that now represents the letter *s* in Morse code. Their origin is still a mystery, as is the reason why they fluctuated with the position of the planet Mars.

The tesla is actually a unit of magnetic flux density which describes the number of lines of magnetic force which will thread an area of a square metre held perpendicular to the lines.

This is not quite the same as a unit of field strength, but from our point of view we can use the tesla as a measure of how strong magnetism is.

You can best understand how large a unit of magnetism the tesla is when I say that the strongest magnets you can buy at the ironmonger's produce only fractions of a tesla. A really strong industrial or research magnet may generate about a single tesla. I once had one of these for a research project and, after the conclusion of the project, kept the magnet to prove to my students how strong magnetism can be. What I did was to get a big iron retort stand and let it clamp on to the magnet. Then I would ask one of the strong young men to pull it off. No one could do it with a direct pull; they managed only by twisting it off, or using some such approach.

Superconductors

My calculated field at the saucer worked out to be a million teslas! Magnetism is radiated when electric current flows, and such large fields would certainly be possible if we could get rid of electrical resistance – which we can. If we refrigerate certain metals at very low temperatures, they lose all their electrical resistance and can carry immense amounts of electric current. They are called superconductors, and electrical engineers are working on superconducting cables for transferring power with none of the losses that occur with ordinary power lines.

However, the need to refrigerate the conductors is a great practical drawback and much research is being done into the development of superconductors which do not need to be refrigerated. As someone has pointed out, we all have one: the brain. The brain seems to be able to process a vast quantity of electromagnetic signals without any form of heat being generated. Such superconductors will need to be new materials altogether – the kind of materials that our meagre knowledge of the structure of flying saucers leads us to believe could be used in their manufacture.

Big, Big Currents

It is an incontrovertible law of nature that magnetism is only generated when electric currents flow and so large magnetic fields indicate large electric currents. What if the magnite-sandwich construction of the bell surface of a flying saucer is made of superconducting sheets? Then we could have a vast electric current flowing in the sandwich.

I worked out what that current might have to amount to and found that it was still feasible if the UFOnauts had developed superconductors which operated at normal temperatures. At the same time, I was working towards the same conclusion from another angle. Was this electric current the source of the force that gave the UFO its remarkable performance?

Certainly, however we figure it, there is a vast amount of EM energy surrounding saucers, and while the UFOnauts may be using subtle techniques, they cannot go against the universal laws of nature. The radiation of magnetism is an absolutely certain sign of the flow of electric current, so whatever powers any UFO that radiates magnetism, it has to have big currents flowing in it. This, it may be argued, is possibly a spin-off from its main means of propulsion, and I cannot deny that possibility, but I decided to consider it the result of the UFOs' main power source and go on delving into the consequences.

The Problem of Silence

Perhaps the feature that makes people most incredulous about UFOs is their silence. They perform the most amazing manoeuvres and yet they usually make no noise. We cannot help contrasting that with the cacophony of a space rocket blasting off. The rocket makes its din because it is using very hot molecules to get the reaction that will force it into space. Molecules in motion can affect other molecules and so the air, which is after all only molecules, conducts the pressure waves from the rocket efflux to those watching, who may need to have their hands over their ears.

Silence when vast power is in use must involve reaction from particles which are thousands of times less massive than molecules, and we have such a particle all about us – the electron. The electron is so much smaller than any molecule that it cannot make the latter move when the two collide. So there can be no sound when electrons impinge on things. This is a very telling reason why the propulsion system of the UFO has to be on the electronic – that is, sub-atomic – scale. At the same time, all our knowledge of UFOs indicates that their propulsion system is internal.

The rocket works only because it ejects a vast mass of gases at very high speed. In other words, it pollutes the atmosphere in which it finds itself. The UFO does not do that. Its method of propulsion is internal and only the aura that surrounds it has any real effect on its surroundings. Where UFOs land there may be scorched patches of grass or other vegetation, and sometimes indentations where landing gear has rested, but there is no sign of the burnt-up areas there would be if the craft were propelled in any way by a rocket-like system.

There is a piece of apparatus found in many schools where A-level physics is taught that consists of a finely balanced set of mica paddles fixed like the spokes of a wheel on an axle. This axle is free to run along low-friction rails and the whole thing is set in a glass tube from which much of the air has been extracted. The paddles are arranged to intercept a stream of electrons flowing between two electrodes and the force of the electrons hitting the faces of the paddles in turn makes the wheel rotate and run along the rails. The object is to demonstrate in as convincing a way as possible that electrons have momentum and so can exert mechanical force when they hit something put in their way.

Having demonstrated this apparatus dozens of times, I began to think it possible that maybe, if there was a large electric current flowing in the saucer's bell surface, then perhaps its purpose was to provide a lifting force. This force could then be within the material of the bell surface, which might appear to be lifting itself. Was the flying carpet quite so fantastic an idea? I decided to do some calculations to find out, and also to invoke some of the more quirky modern scientific ideas that have surfaced since Einstein propounded his famous equations stemming from his theories of relativity.

Before we can make much further progress, we are going to have to explain some of the amazing things that modern physics has thrown at us in the last seventy years.

CHAPTER
6

Why Antimatter?

ONE OF the publishing success stories of recent years has been Professor Stephen Hawking's book about the 'Big Bang' theory, *A Brief History of Time* (1988). This might seem an unlikely best-seller, but that is exactly what it became. Obviously, whether they understand any of it or not, the general public find discussion about the origins of the universe immensely interesting. Hawking has tried to explain the modern cosmologists' view that the universe as we see it today is the remains of a primeval 'explosion'. In the beginning, so the theory goes, there was a total void – no space, no matter in that space and so no time, as there was nothing by which time could be measured. Then, for inexplicable reasons, an immensely small, unbelievably dense lump of energy appeared in that void and exploded. Only after the briefest of moments in the universe's early history matter was born. During that initial moment many, many other things happened, and one of them was the creation of antimatter along with the matter. As this early instant progressed, an imbalance in the physical effects led to the loss of the antimatter, leaving only the matter to go on and form the universe as we see it today: a universe controlled by its own gravity, where clumps of stars forming the island universes we call galaxies move outwards from the centre, where the 'Big Bang' occurred, and the further they are from that centre the faster they are travelling. A weak radiation background still exists, between the galaxies and the stars of the galaxies, which is thought to be the whisper of the original, immensely 'hot', exploding universe. Strictly speaking, you would expect deep space to be absolutely cold: its temperature ought to be the –273 degrees Celsius which is the absolute zero of temperature. Nothing can be colder than absolute zero, yet space sends us radiation which tells us that its temperature is a few degrees above absolute zero. It is clues like this that make feasible the strange idea of a universe starting as a 'Big Bang'.

It would appear that our 'home' galaxy is a more or less normal sort of galaxy, and the sun is a fairly average star in a fairly average position in the mainstream of the disc of stars that form the galaxy. This would seem to indicate that we are in a good position to be a point of call for space races, who must occupy the planets of the stars that surround us.

Gary Kinder, in his book *Light Years* (1987), describes his contact with an Austrian, Eduard Meier, who claims he had meetings over several years with beings from the Pleiades. In *Alien Contact*, Jenny Randles and Paul Whetnall (1981) describe the remarkable Sunderland family's contact with space denizens: the family even knew the names of two of the entities encountered, as well as the name of the planet from which they came. Information from the aliens themselves says that there are inhabited planets out in space and those who occupy some of them are very advanced in many ways compared to us, while in others it would appear that they envy us, and even need our solid earthiness.

However, we must return to antimatter. Modern physics has re-created the conditions of the 'Big Bang' through powerful particle-smashers called proton-synchrotrons. At the same time, it has been established that every fundamental particle has a mirror image of itself called an antiparticle. The billions of dollars that have been spent in creating these giant circular 'racetracks' for protons have led to a model of nature which goes way beyond the real world as we see it.

When a proton is accelerated up to energies of billions of electronvolts and strikes another proton or neutron, then what is being re-created is the collision of those same particles in the early moments of the 'Big Bang'. Many, many things then happen, including the creation of super-heavy particles called hyperons, which have not been seen since the 'Big Bang' created them ten to fifteen billion years ago. Hyperons – and all other exotic particles – transform into other particles almost as soon as they are created, and so do their antiparticles, but the end products of the decays and transformations that occur are always the same. They are protons, neutrons and electrons – the stable building-blocks out of which all the atoms are made. There is also one other ingredient of immense importance – photons of electromagnetic energy. So where can we find antimatter today?

There are almost as many antiparticle types as there are particles, but we are going to be interested in only one antiparticle and that is the positron – the antiparticle of the electron. We can get streams of positrons from certain radioactive isotopes and as long as we do not allow them near electrons, then positrons will exist for ever. However, when a positron meets an electron, the result is a 'Little Bang'. Both the electron and the positron disappear and from where they met come two gamma photons. We say the electron and positron have 'annihilated', and in simple terms matter has been destroyed.

Conversely, under the right circumstances, and sometimes spontaneously, a gamma photon with enough energy will vanish and transform into an electron and a positron. Here matter has been created, but it could not have been created without antimatter being created at the same time – which would seem to go against the fundamental law that matter can neither be created nor destroyed. However, in the view of modern physics the law is wrongly stated. What it should say is that the mass-energy of the universe cannot be changed.

To understand the term 'mass-energy' we have to go back to Einstein, who showed through his famous mass-energy relation ($E = mc^2$) that mass (m) is just 'frozen' energy (E). Given the right conditions, we can unfreeze mass and turn it into energy. In the case of electrons which annihilate with positrons, the energy will always be in the form of gamma photons. The mass-energy involved in this transformation is a million electronvolts (MeV). Because of its overriding importance in describing energy changes, we must explain this electronvolt unit.

The electronvolt (eV) is a unit tailored to give meaning to the changes in energy involved when electrons in atoms shift their orbits. Whenever light is seen, the source of that light has stemmed from changes in the energy levels of electrons. Those electrons are usually in orbits about the nuclei of atoms, molecules, etc., but they do not have to be.

The principles by which light is created can be understood with a model of the simplest atom – hydrogen. Hydrogen has a single electron whirling in a spherical orbit about a single proton which forms its nucleus (Fig. 6.1). In any atom an electron which takes part in the emission of light from the atom is called an 'optical electron'.

If it is not disturbed, the orbit of the optical electron in a hydrogen atom is an angstrom unit across. The angstrom unit is one ten-billionth of a metre, but as that is impossible to conceive let us say that the angstrom is a unit tailored to describe the size of atoms and molecules. If the smallest atom (hydrogen) has a diameter of one angstrom, then all the others must be bigger and have diameters of a few angstroms. For example, an atom of the gas argon (with eighteen electrons) has a diameter of 3.5 angstroms.

The practical way to make atoms emit light is to put them in a tube at pressures of around a thousandth of normal atmospheric pressure. This 'discharge tube' is fitted with a positive and a negative electrode and very high voltage is applied across the electrodes. This results in most of the atoms having electrons knocked off them. But electrons do not like the loneliness of being

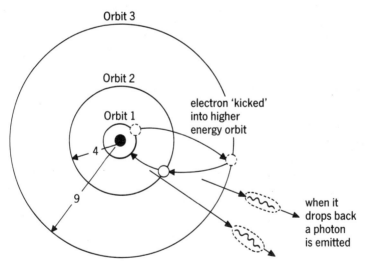

Fig. 6.1 How electron 'jumps' in an atom lead to the emission of a spectrum of light. The electron normally stays in Orbit 1, but if energized into a higher orbit it has to fall back, leading to photons of definite wavelength which are characteristic of that atom. All emissions of light are due to electrons changing their energies in one way or another.

outside atoms and always strive to recombine. As they do so, they emit the light and other radiations which are characteristic of the atoms in the tube. We see such tubes used for signs and street and motorway lighting.

So let us assume that we have hydrogen in a discharge tube. Whenever the electron in one of the hydrogen atoms finds itself in, say, Orbit 3, it may drop down into Orbit 2, but when it does so the result is that a photon of red light is emitted. Then the electron will drop back to Orbit 1, from where it starts this time emitting a photon of ultraviolet light. The electron will, just like a ball thrown up an irregular flight of stairs, always be trying to get back to its familiar 'ground' orbit. If you wonder why the electron cannot occupy any old orbit, then the answer lies in the fact that only certain orbital energies are allowed in any particular atom. The number of orbits may be very large with complicated atoms, but they are always discrete.

There are many, many orbits higher than the ones we have chosen for this explanation. Yet in exactly the same way as already described, the hydrogen atom gives out a spectrum of photons the wavelengths of which are a fingerprint of that atom. All other atoms will give different emissions.

To take a familar example, the intense yellow light from street lamps is due to changes in the orbit of an optical electron in sodium atoms. These 'quantum jumps' of the optical electron in the tube of the sodium lamp are produced by collision between atoms of sodium vapour. As vast numbers of sodium atoms are in violent motion within the lamp, so vast numbers of photons bathe the surroundings in just one colour – sodium yellow. The spectrum of photons to which our eyes can react possesses energies that must lie between 3 eV at the violet end to about 1.5 eV at the red end and everything you have ever seen has come to you via photons in that very narrow band of electromagnetic energies. The sodium-yellow photons just mentioned each have an energy of 2 eV – close to the middle of the visible spectrum and an energy to which, incidentally, the human eye is very sensitive.

When we realize that the electromagnetic energy spectrum ranges from radio waves, where the energies are millionths of an eV, to gamma rays, with energies of millions of eV, then a span of a few eV is a very small window through which to observe the world

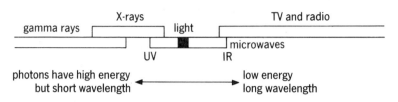

Fig. 6.2 The electromagnetic (EM) spectrum.

around us (Fig. 6.2). So believing may not always come from seeing. However, it is certain that when you see a UFO shining in the sky the processes which are producing the light involve common old electrons changing their energy levels within that very narrow band of 1.5 to 3 eV. There is no other way!

It is worth noting for explanations we will come to later that for electromagnetic waves wavelength × photon energy always equals the same quantity. Thus short waves (i.e. gamma and X-rays) have high energy and long waves (radio, TV, infra-red) correspondingly low energy. Which means their individual photons have these energies. We all know that a radio station must broadcast its waves at energies vastly greater than an X-ray machine will do. It is just that in the former case the photons co-operate to produce waves of very great power, despite their long wavelength. In the case of light from street lamps and light bulbs, the photons do not co-operate and come to you as a stream of minute packets of waves (photons), all individual but still hopelessly jumbled up. Only in laser light do the photons co-operate and that is why a laser has such great power in comparison with other sources of light.

Although it has not been proved, it seems very likely that beams of light which emanate from UFOs are often in the form of laser light. However, I believe that in some cases they are complex beams made up of different components which may interfere with one another, so that an action of some kind can occur where the beams intersect (we will see an example of this later). Further, the beams are often described as clear-cut, so that the division between the beam and its surroundings is quite sharp. This is what we find also with laser light and it indicates a very intense electromagnetic 'strain' in the space through which the light is travelling.

What's in a Vacuum?

How can apparently empty space be 'strained'? Certainly the effect has nothing to do with air: the beams would look just the same in space. To understand this, we must take on board the modern physicist's view of a vacuum – which is not at all empty!

Only with the aid of antimatter can a vacuum have an apparent emptiness and yet be teeming with physical life. All total vacuum means is that there is no apparent matter there – no atoms, no ions (atoms, molecules, etc. with electric charge) – but there are still immense numbers of electrons. So shouldn't a vacuum be incredibly highly charged? It would be were it not for positrons equal in number to the electrons. The positrons cancel most of the effects of the electrons.

To visualize a vacuum you have to stretch your imagination and think of a lump of wholly empty space. Then, in this total void, imagine the sudden creation of an electron and a positron together (an e–p pair). Now you have not changed the universe much. You have not, for instance, created more electric charge, because the positive positron cancels the negative electron. You have not introduced more magnetism, because the two particles spin in opposite directions and produce magnetism that also cancels. You seem to have increased mass/energy, but the time for which the pair exists is very, very short – too short to be recognized by any normal measurement technique – after which they recombine.

Think of your bit of space as full of these electron-positron pairs, constantly evolving and annihilating, forming a sea of agitation. Now imagine all apparently empty space filled with this boiling assemblage of matter and antimatter. Allow it to fill the space between the galaxies, between the stars of those galaxies, and hide within the atoms of the planets of those stars. In fact, anywhere light can travel the electron-positron 'sea' must exist. For the 'sea' is the medium which, being itself electric and magnetic, oscillates to transport the electromagnetic waves that are the photons. So it must fill the whole of space or we could not see the galaxies that send us light from the edges of the universe.

Just as the ordinary watery sea transports energy by water waves, so the e-p sea transports energy by electromagnetic waves. Water waves may travel at a few tens of miles an hour, but electromagnetic waves always travel at 3×10^8 (300 million) metres per second. That means about twenty-four times the diameter of earth in the time you can say 'one-and'.

So, must it be totally impossible for Meier's alien contacts to have come from the Pleiades, which are over 400 light-years away? Such a distance means that the light we get from the Pleiades today left there when Queen Elizabeth I was nearing the end of her reign and William Shakespeare was hard at it, writing his plays.

Certainly, with our restricted knowledge of science, we might imagine that it is impossible. However, we are still stuck with Einstein's theories, which state that the mass of humans and machines travelling at the speed of light must be infinitely large but say nothing about things which can travel faster. Scientists study particles that can travel faster than light and call them 'tachyons'. So science has begun to recognize a world beyond Einstein, and just as Einstein updated Newton, so 'Professor X' will one day update Einstein. That day may be still far away, but until it comes we must grab whatever crumbs of knowledge we can from the visitors themselves.

Andrija Puharich in his book *Uri* (1974), describes how, on the evening of 31 December 1952, he recorded the 'automatic speech' of Dr D. G. Vinod, a Hindu scholar and sage from Poona, India. Vinod entered a trance state and delivered a ninety-minute statement, not in his own high-pitched, soft voice but in a deep, sonorous tone and also in perfect English, without an accent. The statement came from entities calling themselves 'M', who stated that they were 'nine principles and forces, personalities if you will, working in complete mutual implication'. In the course of the statement, 'M' through Vinod tells us that if the Einstein/Lorentz equation is put equal to 7, then, 'that is the point where human personality has to be stretched in order to achieve infinitization'. Now the Einstein/Lorentz equation is the one which enables us to calculate the increase in the mass of a body as it gets closer and closer to the speed of light.

From solving the equation and reading between the lines, I interpret this statement as meaning that when the speed of a conscious body approaches 90 per cent of the speed of light, a change comes over it and it then enters a new realm the attributes of which are, as yet, unknown to us. However, other passages in the testimony of 'M' indicate that here we are in the 'transfer world', where what are considered at present to be uncontrolled psychic phenomena can come under control. To quote from *Uri*:

> The whole group of concepts has to be revised. The problem of psychokinesis, clairvoyance, etc., at the present stage is all right, but profoundly misleading . . . Soon we will come to basic universal categories of explicating the superconscious.

When Meier (Kinder, 1987) was transported to the home planet of his contact, it apparently took three and a half hours to achieve the 'transfer' speed and a similar length of time to decelerate down from it, while the intermediate translation took only a few seconds, if that.

In most accounts of contact with aliens – and a large body of evidence now exists in this field – there is overwhelming proof that things we consider to be purely psychic and therefore beyond our reason can be under the conscious control of the alien mind. If this is impossible to accept, then we have only to consider what scientists thought about things in 1900. There was no atomic theory, no quantum theory. Newton had proposed the idea of corpuscles like photons, but he never managed to get as far as making his electromagnetic waves into little packets. For over 200 years the science of light went forward imagining that atoms gave out continuous strings of waves. Scientific progress did not, in that era, need those strings chopped up into short lengths, as the quantum theory did.

No one in 1900 knew anything about the atomic nucleus, much less about exotic ideas like antimatter. To suggest that we could, as has been done, make anti-atoms by combining anti-nucleons with anti-electrons and so seriously posit the idea that there could be an anti-universe, where all the particles were antiparticles, would have been laughed out of court, even if anyone had the imagination to conceive of it. Interestingly, the only thing that can commute between our own and an anti-universe is light, because light is as happy to be created or accepted by anti-atoms as it is by atoms. An anti-hydrogen atom gives out exactly the same spectrum of light as an ordinary hydrogen atom; again, this has been proved scientifically.

What has also been proved scientifically is that the light from all atoms, including hydrogen atoms, comes in individual, well-spaced wavelengths, as each kind of atom gives out its own characteristic 'fingerprint' of wavelengths. So, we know that the atoms familiar to us on earth are in the auras of distant stars and that exactly the same matter builds the whole of the visible universe.

In particular, everywhere we look there is hydrogen. Further, the wavelengths of the light hydrogen emits have been measured to a remarkable degree of accuracy. It is probably the most studied spectrum of them all. Yet the accurately measured wavelengths show a slight 'wobble', due to the atom's electron being 'jostled' by the electron-positron pairs created all about it as it gyrates in its otherwise perfectly 'empty' little shell of space. This leads scientists to believe that their matter-antimatter 'sea' is more than just a figment of the scientific mind and they can work out the consequences. The UFOs work in this sea just as much as we do, but they may have found ways of manipulating it that we have not yet even contemplated, let alone mastered.

Hopefully, the foregoing is enough to convince the reader that antimatter is as much accepted by science as is matter. In fact, our modern scientific edifice could not stand without it, and its strange properties might have a lot to do with the way some, if not all, UFOs are propelled. We will propose certain ideas along these lines in the next chapter.

CHAPTER
7

The Saucer – a Universal Flying Carpet

ONE OF the most interesting facets of George Adamski's pictures of the saucer he encountered is its aura. In Photo 6 in *Flying Saucers Have Landed* (Leslie and Adamski, 1953), there is a distinct sheet of light covering the upper surface and another lesser one ringing the top of the cupola. The caption tells us that this picture differs from the others because the craft was then rising. In other words, it had turned on power to lift away and, at the same time, move sideways. The caption to the frontispiece tells us that the spacecraft was made of a 'translucent metal' – words for which the schoolboy Stephen Darbishire was searching with his more limited vocabulary when he described the similar craft he photographed fifteen months later near Coniston Old Man. There are good scientific reasons to explain why this apparent translucence is not of the saucer's skin but is an effect of its force field. However, we must consider some other problems first.

It is not generally realized that Adamski was not the only one to get a picture of the saucer. Photo 7 in *Flying Saucers Have Landed* was taken a few moments later than Photo 6 by Sergeant Jerrold E. Baker with a Kodak Brownie camera as the saucer passed rapidly over the low hill on which he was standing. The caption reads: 'The blurred effect is due to the rapid speed at which the craft was moving.' But this may not be true, any more than bad focusing explained the fuzzy appearance of Stephen Darbishire's picture.

Let There be Light

I think I know the possible origin of the aura that builds only when the craft's power system begins to develop lift and drive. It is a light source known since 1947, when it was first seen in an electron synchrotron used by GEC in America (Glasstone, 1958). Today 'synchrotron radiation' has been developed from what was originally a nuisance into a means of obtaining extremely intense beams of photons for research purposes. Synchrotron radiation can produce high-intensity beams of EM radiation right across the spectrum, from infra-red to high-energy gamma rays, and that, of course, includes visible light (Winick, 1987).

Synchrotrons whirl electrons around to high energies and they use powerful magnets to bend the beams into circular paths. The interaction of the electrons with the magnetic lines of force means that the equivalent of atoms are formed, with the electrons making little circular orbits about the magnetic lines (Fig. 7.1). If the magnetic fields are strong, then the electrons will rotate in circles that are, as an example, as small as a hydrogen atom. As the magnetic field or the speed of the electrons changes, so photons of a whole spectrum of colours can be given out. Increase the magnetic field and the colours emitted will shift from red through to violet and beyond into the invisible realms of ultraviolet (giving sunburn-like effects), as well as X-rays and gamma rays. There is some evidence to suggest that the colours emitted by UFOs go from red to white through violet as the craft accelerate.

The UFOs have strong magnetic fields about them and, in all probability, masses of electrons around their surfaces as well. These are both the requirements for strong synchrotron radiation and so, when UFOs shine, they may not be doing so because they want to but because they cannot help it. Synchrotron light from UFOs can occur anywhere, but in the atmosphere there will also be extra light from ionized air which will glow just as discharge lighting does – by electrons and ionized molecules of air colliding with one another.

This form of light occurs naturally and can be seen on many nights in Scotland and on similar northern latitudes. It is the aurora borealis, or the 'northern lights', the southern hemisphere equivalent of which is the aurora australis. These bands and

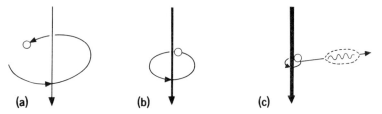

Fig. 7.1 We do not have to have atoms to make electrons orbit and send out light. Free electrons will naturally form orbits about magnetic lines of force. **(a)** A weak magnetic field leads to electrons spinning in large orbits. **(b)** Increasing the field makes the orbits tighten into smaller circles. **(c)** A very intense field leads to the electrons' orbits becoming as small as those in atoms. Small variations in the magnetism will then lead to the emission of synchrotron radiation, which can be highly visible, as well as emitting invisible rays.

sheets of pastel colours ring the hemisphere and are caused by electrons from the sun whirling in from space to collide with molecules of air in the high atmosphere. When there are particularly active 'storms' on the sun, the 'great aurora' may spread southwards as far as the tropics; otherwise you have to go to Canada, Scandinavia, etc. to be sure of seeing it.

We saw in the last chapter how quantum jumps (with energies in the very narrow band of about 1.5 to 3 eV) must lead to visible light being emitted. UFOs with strong magnetic fields – which may mean most UFOs – must therefore radiate synchrotron radiation both visible and invisible. However, this is not the only possible source of UFO light.

As long ago as 1934 a Russian physicist, P. A. Cerenkov, showed that water and glass both gave out blue-white light when high energy rays went through them. In 1937 this strange blue light was shown to be the EM equivalent of the sonic bang heard when an aircraft goes through the sound barrier. In the latter case, as the aircraft tries to part the air at a speed greater than it naturally wants to go (which is the speed of sound), the air piles up on to a shock wave which, when it passes you, gives the sonic bang (Fig. 7.2). Similarly, when electrons going at speeds close to that of light – and it does not take much energy to make them go that fast – enter, say, glass, in which the speed of light is slower than in air, they create a shock wave and from that shock wave

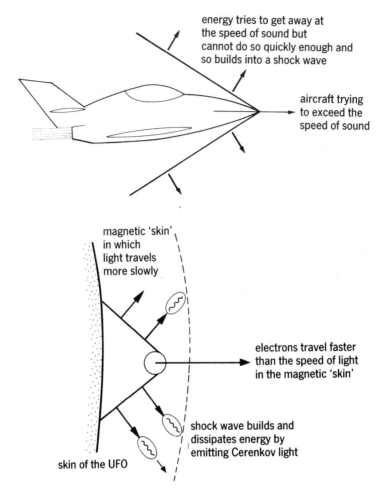

energy tries to get away at
the speed of sound but
cannot do so quickly enough and
so builds into a shock wave

aircraft trying
to exceed the
speed of sound

magnetic 'skin'
in which
light travels
more slowly

electrons travel faster
than the speed of light
in the magnetic 'skin'

shock wave builds and
dissipates energy by
emitting Cerenkov light

skin of the UFO

Fig. 7.2   The analogy between a supersonic aircraft trying to crash the sound barrier and an electron moving close to the speed of light: in the former case the result is a sonic bang; in the latter, blue Cerenkov radiation.

stems the so-called Cerenkov radiation. As we will see, there is every reason for expecting UFOs to emit Cerenkov radiation.

We must not forget that there will be forms of light that the UFO denizens choose to use themselves. So, there are several ways in which UFOs can emit light and it is very likely that, when you see a bright UFO, any or all of them could be there. But of them all the most intense is almost certainly going to be synchrotron light. I think it is synchrotron light that was flushing across the bell surface of Adamski's saucer as it wound up its power for take-off. This prompts the question, 'What power source could lead to these effects?' But before we give any kind of answer to that, we must ask another question: 'Why the saucer?'

We need a theory that answers some of the following questions:

Why is an inverted saucer the best shape for a spacecraft?

How could a relatively thin surface like the curved surface of a saucer lift itself without external assistance?

How could such a system emit strong magnetism and yet not appear to leave any residual traces of magnetism in metal objects near it?

How could the bell surface of a saucer seen on the ground appear to be rotating while the cupola remained stationary, as has been reported on a number of occasions?

Possible answers to these, and other conundrums, follow.

The Shape of the Saucer

You could get close to the reported performance of UFOs of the classic inverted-saucer shape with a lift-to-drive ratio of about 5:1. What that means is illustrated in Fig. 7.3. Let us imagine that all we want to do is to create a force that will go straight up (a). This means that over a disc we are going to have to generate a force from inside its surface. For reasons that will become apparent, we will call this the 'bell force'.

Assume that this bell force works along the lengths of four 'lift arms' which rotate from the centre of the disc. Rotating these at a reasonably rapid rate will provide a stable lift. So, if going up against gravity is all we want to do, the flat disc would be adequate.

However, we also want to go sideways and so, as in (b), we can get sideways force in any desired direction by ensuring that the lift arm wraps round the side of a shape that looks like the lid of

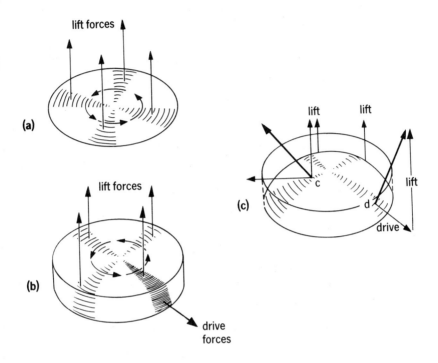

Fig. 7.3 Why a saucer? The answer may lie in the UFOs' ability not only to defy gravity but also to move in any sideways direction at will.

an old-fashioned cocoa tin. We can now call this part a 'drive arm'. Every time a drive arm goes past the desired direction, the drive force is increased there, allowing the device to go in the desired direction.

But why make it like that when you could achieve the same result with the classic saucer shape (c)? Measuring the relative dimensions of Adamski's saucer shows that the 5:1 ratio is about right.

Now, the bell force from a force arm will be perpendicular to the surface – upright near the cupola and more horizontal near the rim. The total force resolves itself into a horizontal-drive component plus a vertical-lift component, but it will work just like the cocoa-tin shape only better.

Here we have a reason for the classic saucer shape: it is the right shape for a universal flying device the motive power of which lies in its inverted-saucer-shaped skin. It will also provide the correct performance characteristics and you can accelerate off in any direction at will.

In the case of Bernard Miserey's observation at Vernon (Chapter 2), the saucers that fell out of the bottom of the vertical Leviathan slowed and then 'wobbled' before shooting off. This has been observed many, many times when saucers arrest themselves after freefall. This would, in the context of rotating force arms, be the way you would expect them to act. For first of all the full effect of lift forces has to be used to counteract gravity with no drive in any particular direction. Then, as the drive arms begin to rotate, force builds in one direction, but before it is fully established, there will be a small sideways force which will cause the characteristic wobble. It is like a wheel with a slight imbalance: when it first begins to rotate it will vibrate, often alarmingly; then, as the speed builds, it settles down to steady motion.

Dynamics of the Saucer

Because it is the only type of which we have detailed knowledge, we must take Adamski's saucer as our example (Fig. 7.4). In (a) we show the craft hovering. The bell forces resolve into lift and sideways force. They are shown by broken lines because you have not got three forces here: you can either have the (solid) arrow for bell force or take that away and replace it with the two other broken components. The lift forces are adjusted to just equal the weight of the saucer and then the sideways forces cancel each other as they are pushing equally in opposite directions.

Now let us assume that we want to go to the right. Every time the force arms go past that direction, the force is suddenly strengthened. The bell-force arrow gets a good deal longer, which means its components get bigger. Increased drive is what we want, but we get increased lift as well. That will tend to make the saucer rotate (d) about its centre of mass (M), so that it will up-end in the direction of flight. The UFOnauts may find that useful at the moment they move off, as it directs the saucer skywards, but left to itself, it will have the device looping the loop.

There has to be a counteracting force and this is where the light band above the cupola could come in, indicating, as it does, that drive power is there. If, as in (b), a 'cupola drive' is added, it will have a counteracting effect (c) and varying this will stabilize the craft in the direction it wants to go. This cupola drive force would have the same function as the tail rotor of a helicopter, preventing the craft turning about its own axis as it flies.

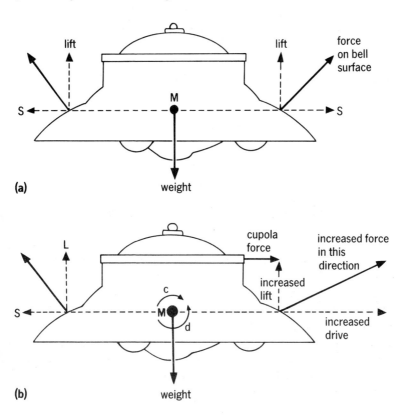

Fig. 7.4 Saucer dynamics. **(a)** This shows the balanced forces when hovering. Lift is the same all round and balances weight, while the sideways forces (S) cancel each other. **(b)** If the bell-force idea is right, there will be an imbalance of forces as the saucer accelerates away. This has to be corrected by an opposing cupola force. Evidence for such a force appears in several of Adamski's pictures.

Now, I know that there are a host of problems to be solved with a suggestion such as this, but at least it is beginning to throw up answers to questions that other suggestions I have read in the past do not. Let's go on and ask how we could achieve the forces anyway. This will answer other aspects of the way saucers are seen to behave.

The Flying-carpet Idea

Every scientific theory has to have an origin. Most of them are basic ideas that no one fully understands but everyone accepts. Mechanics need the idea of mass and yet mass is one of the most mysterious quantities anyone could work with. It would seem to be immutable, but it can be changed into energy; it varies with the speed it travels and it would be different if the universe were different.

The whole edifice of electricity stands on the idea of electric charge, but the most advanced treatises on the subject have to start with an article of faith: 'Electric charge exists.' No one is very sure what electric charge is. No one has ever seen an electron and so we have enormous visual problems with theories which demand that at one moment an electron be thought of as a snooker ball and at another as a wave. If you could stick a label on an electron and call it 'Fred', then it is most likely that Fred would exist only for a minute fraction of a second before being replaced by its identical twin, 'Tom'. The stream of electrons that travel down your TV tube can most easily be visualized as a succession of small spheres, each with a 'minus' label on it striking the inside of the screen. An image that fits modern ideas better has a strange pinball machine with a set of holes along the beam. A ball drops into a hole and immediately another identical ball shoots out and into the next hole down the line, and so on until at the end of the line the last electron activates the screen, but it is not the electron with which we started.

However, as all electrons look alike, the simple ideas are best to help with understanding, even if they do not fully fit the modern theories.

To come up with a theory for a self-lifting bell surface we have, just as with other theories, to make certain assumptions, based on solid reason. The advanced UFO technologists must have developed the following things that we have not yet been able to do:

very tough, light metal-like materials which are super-conductors (Strieber, 1990);

a way of allowing electron-positron pairs to be produced without the expenditure of a million eV of energy every time a pair is created.

If we accept that they can have done these things, then we also need a device which I am going to call a 'gamma gun'. Remembering the construction of the Silpho Moor object, we imagine (Fig. 7.5) that the gamma gun rotates round and looks into the magnite sandwich, which forms the bell surface of the saucer. It shoots in gamma photons, which, interacting with the insulating 'filling' of the sandwich, produce copious numbers of e-p pairs, which shoot off down the filling. This, however, is permeated by a magnetic field which makes the electrons curve upwards (Fig. 7.6), while the positrons curve downwards. This accentuates the magnetic field and maintains the separation of the particles.

However, because the positrons are antimatter, they annihilate with the first electron they find in the filling or the lower superconducting surface. The result is gamma radiation of energy half a million eV each – only half that required to create new e-p pairs. We will come to the fate of these gammas in the next chapter.

The most important point – and this is why antimatter is an absolutely vital part of the process – is that no force is exerted by the positrons when, going downwards, they annihilate with electrons, but a force is exerted upwards by the electrons. The result is a lifting force and no corresponding downwards force. Action and reaction are not now equal and opposite.

We now see why the surfaces of the Silpho Moor magnite sandwich were joined electrically at the rim. The electrons have to be cleared away from the upper superconducting surface and returned to the lower surface so as to replace the electrons that are being annihilated by the positrons. This is why there is such a vast electric current flowing in the bell surfaces and a correspondingly vast magnetic field around the saucer. The high electrical potential this will generate would lead to a small electric storm of discharge

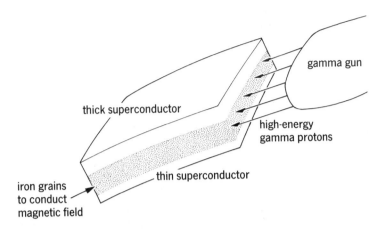

Fig. 7.5 This shows the magnite sandwich. Based on the construction of the Silpho Moor object, the rotating gamma guns would create an internal lift when they shot electron-positron pairs down the 'filling' of the magnite sandwich.

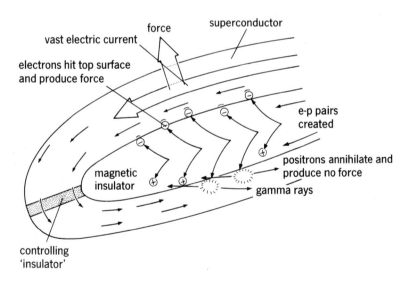

Fig. 7.6 How the force could apply upwards and outwards, but there would be no corresponding force downwards, as the antimatter positrons would annihilate with the electrons in the lower layers of the sandwich. The resulting gamma rays would be contained by the saucer's own magnetic sheath.

between the bell surface and the cupola if the otherwise abrupt join was not faired in in the way that it is in Adamski's saucer (see Fig. 5.1).

Doing the Sums

When I thought this out, the theory seemed to fit many of the facts, but could it really form a propulsion system? Was it possible that, provided there were sufficient e-p pairs, it could give a force of sufficient magnitude to power a saucer?

When I did the sums, I was surprised to find that the kind of electric current which would create the magnetic field I had previously calculated was also about right to provide the force which could give the saucer an acceleration of 10 G – i.e. ten times the 10 metres per second per second experienced by a body in free fall near earth. That, I considered, was enough. It would not allow a saucer to go so fast as to disappear before your very eyes, but other aspects of the theory were going to make sudden invisibility possible.

Certain cases on record indicate that some saucers broadcast alternating magnetic fields. The Vins-sur-Caramy case of 15 April 1957 is reported by Alan Hynek (1972). Two elderly French women were walking along a road when a curious metallic machine landed in the road some 300 yd ahead of them. It was in the form of 'a large children's top'. As it landed, a large metallic sign some 15–20 ft from the craft was set into violent vibration, which created a deafening rattle. A little later the craft jumped off the road and landed a second time, but on a road that forked from the previous one. It had to fly over another road sign and this too was set into sudden motion with, to quote a witness, 'violent shocks repeated in rapid cadence'. The machine itself made no sound – which, from what we now understand about the propulsion system of saucers, is not surprising.

The local police considered the action to be connected to magnetism radiated by the device, for they placed a compass near to the two signs and found a deviation of some 15 degrees, although there was no deviation at all close to a third sign which was much further from the object throughout the encounter. They tested their compass near their own Renault car as a 'control' metal object and found only a 4-degree deviation.

We have stated elsewhere that metallic objects will be demagnetized because of the slow diminution of the alternating magnetic field as the UFO moves away. In this case the object 'jumped' and so could have left magnetism in the signs, just as we do to magnetize a piece of steel, suddenly switching off alternating currents passing through a surrounding solenoid, leaving the ferrous metal magnetized one way or the other.

In the case of the saucer which paced Ronald Wildman's car (see page 51), UFO researchers tested the surroundings for magnetism and found none. At the time, they therefore thought this meant that the magnetic-field theory of UFO interference with cars was wrong. Of course, to leave no magnetic residue, as well as no other lasting physical signs, is just how the UFOnauts want it, and would be the natural consequence of an alternating magnetic field produced by rotating force arms as envisaged above.

The ideas being proposed here are only a small contribution to our understanding of the way the advanced space races work. It is something we can just about understand, whereas other things that happen in the presence of UFOS are, as yet, beyond our comprehension. Some people who have been temporarily abducted by the UFOnauts describe, under hypnotic regression, how they were 'floated' up into a UFO. We even have cases in which cars and other weighty bodies are lifted lightly up into the maws of waiting spacecraft (Hilton, 1993). In other words, the UFOnauts have means of overcoming gravity. Whether such anti-gravity effects are related to the EM effects we are talking about here or are something else entirely, we do not at present know. All we do know is that these things happen to reliable witnesses.

The scientists working on the frontiers of knowledge are working towards a theory that will explain gravity, electro-magnetism and nuclear force under one set of basic equations. They call this the 'Unified Field Theory' (UFT) and just as Newton never got around to photons although he was halfway there, so Einstein worked on UFT but never achieved a breakthrough. It was something ahead of his time, and much research and thinking has had to go on since then to reach our position today. Even now we may not be permitted to have all the secrets UFT will unlock for us and so we must do what we can within the sphere of our limited knowledge. I am not going to go into theories of anti-gravity here, because frankly I do not understand them, but Cramp (1954) gave some good ideas on how gravity drive might be achieved, and the Plantier theories (Michel, 1957) are worth reading. Here I intend to stick with EM effects.

The magnetic field surrounding saucers is capable of being something vastly greater than anything we are used to, even on the frontiers of research. Thus some very unusual things may occur and these can help to explain observations so strange that people reading about them, rather than experiencing them, will curl up in disbelief. That, however, does not make them impossible, as will be seen in the next chapter.

CHAPTER
8

Strange Tricks of the Light

WHEN ROBERT MILLER managed to get his cine camera trained on a ball-shaped light one night he described it as the size of the moon and he gained the kind of evidence for strange UFO behaviour that makes many people simply switch off. And who can blame them?

The moon-sized circle had a bluish halo about it as it moved from north to south across his field of view. It then did an incredible thing – it divided into sections. The film shows the ball developing a larger oblong 'tail'. Twenty frames later, what appears to be three tiny red and blue lights appear on the film, but these fade away while the larger object regains globular form. It has now exchanged its blue glow for a mixture of bluish-green and orange-white halos. Another twenty frames later, the small UFOs reappear at the same time as the large object again separates. Ten frames later, the large device once again has merged into its original shape.

What, in heaven's name, are we looking at here? I think the answer has to be a very large UFO – probably, because of the oblong tail, a Leviathan – only parts of which are visible at any one time. The outer surfaces of big craft like Leviathans are flushed with the ability to develop power. Thus they will create light in various parts by the means suggested in Chapter 7, leaving the rest invisible in the darkness. The red and blue lights are observed on the edges of large UFOs and what they indicate is not certain. Probably the circular light area was in the centre of the craft and was all it needed to maintain whatever it was doing at the time. Then it may have moved or been preparing to move, when power would have switched to one end, leading to the appearance of the 'tail'. However, when this phase was over, that tail-end power was switched back to the centre again. As the power levels minutely changed, the colours that predominated in the auras also changed.

Blue is a colour associated with Leviathans, as testified by the experience of the two DC3 pilots of Eastern Airlines, mentioned in Chapter 2, Clarence Chiles and his co-pilot, John Whitted. That its sides glowed with a dark-blue light which quivered to and fro along the fuselage, much as light wavers back and forth in some forms of discharge tube, indicates Cerenkov radiation. The two rows of glowing patches which emanated an intense light like a magnesium flare indicate synchrotron radiation. The tail that belched 'flames' has been reported sufficiently often for this emanation to be part and parcel of the Leviathan's propulsion system, but what actually constitutes the 'flames' is not evident. Certainly they are not 'chemical' flames as we know them, but are probably some form of visible electromagnetic effect, for the 'flames' dissolved into 'a weird bundle of rays' and there is no way that chemical flames do that.

This happened on the morning of 24 July 1948 and a similar encounter occurred to two other airmen on 30 September 1950. Again they remarked on the double row of 'portholes' and the ethereal blue glow.

The up-ended Leviathan that the vicar of Heytesbury's wife saw near Warminster (see page 21) shared an attribute with the one on the Robert Miller film in that parts of it seemed to be missing. But the answer obviously is that the missing parts are dark and are simply not visible. Here we have partial invisibility caused by the fact that the areas in question are not emitting any light. However, there are cases on record of UFOs, giving strong echoes on radar and in conditions when they should be easily visible, being just totally invisible.

One noon in late September 1954, a British airfield radar picked up a strange U-shaped formation of what appeared to be over forty aircraft. They were on a westerly course at 12,000 ft. The unidentified blips then broke ranks and formed two parallel lines, after which they switched to a Z-shaped formation. Investigation soon showed that they could not be any known aircraft. An inquiry was set up by the Air Ministry, but before it could get under way the formation returned at the same time next day. Both of these days were cloudy and so no visible identification from the ground was possible. On the third day, when the formation returned right on schedule, the sky was clear. Anticipating that there might be another visitation, RAF bases had been put on alert and many radars picked up the ethereal flight as it went through its manoeuvres. Ground observers trained binoculars on the positions where the radars told them the craft should be. Aircraft scrambled to above the height of the formation looked down on where it had to be and saw nothing.

In all, this obviously intelligently controlled visitation occurred at noon on seven consecutive days. Within a month the story had been leaked to the *Sunday Dispatch* and was confirmed by the War Office. Donald Keyhoe (1957) gives a review of this case and, despite the official backing, finds it hard to believe. Yet this is not the only one of its kind. There was also, during the war in the Pacific, the Nansei-shoto riddle.

Towards the end of the war, the US forces were pounding Japanese bases on the Nansei-shoto islands, south of Okinawa. A large radar blip appeared on the radarscope of an aircraft carrier and was given as 120 miles away when it first appeared. It was so large that it represented to the experienced radar operators a formation of at least 200 to 300 aircraft in formation. Rapidly the blip closed to 100 miles and it was heading straight for the carrier at 650 knots – an unbelievable speed for those days. To counter this possible attack, the carrier put up just a dozen fighters – all the aircraft it had available.

When just 80 miles away, the armada spread sideways, embracing the whole task force. The intruders were at 12,000 ft, while the carrier's fighters had climbed to 15,000 ft. Swiftly, the radar blips of friend and apparent foe closed. Then there was consternation in the Combat Information Center of the carrier. As visibility was some 50 miles and their own fighters were above the bogies, why was there no visual contact?

The distance closed to virtually nothing and, despite pleas to look below them, the fighters still saw nothing whatsoever. Equally, as the mystery formation crossed the fleet, no one could see anything either. There was just apparently empty blue sky. In the following weeks, other invisible bogies were tracked on the radars of the US fleet off Okinawa, but there has never been any form of official or unofficial explanation for how objects with enough substance to form large blips on the radar, to manoeuvre like real enemy formations and to have experienced controllers and pilots dumbfounded by the lack of any visual contact could exist (Keyhoe, 1955).

Tricks of Refraction

When you put a stick into a pail of water, the stick apparently bends. As you know it is straight, it does not worry you greatly. You pull out the stick and it is as straight as you expected. But assume that the same thing happened to the stick when you held it out in front of you – no water, no glass, no nothing. You would be very surprised and might well assume that the age of miracles had not passed.

The stick bends in water because refraction makes the light come to you by a different path from the one you expect. You always assume that where you are looking is where the object is, but with refraction things are not always what they seem.

At sunset, when the sun sits on the horizon, it is actually already well below the horizon. The light has been bent round the edge of the earth by refraction through a very long swathe of the atmosphere (Fig. 8.1), but you think the sun is where you are looking and have no way of estimating its true position.

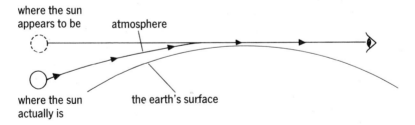

Fig. 8.1 An illustration of how seeing need not necessarily be believing. Near sunset, the sun's rays are curved by refraction in the atmosphere. Thus the true position of the sun is below the horizon, when it still appears to be just setting.

In one of the panes of glass in the dining-room window that looks out into my side garden there is a flaw. I sometimes idly line it up with a thin branch of a tree. The branch appears to have a piece missing in the middle. Now, I'm not worried by that because I know there is a refracting medium – glass – between me and the offending branch. But if I were in the open air and the same thing happened, I would begin to doubt the evidence of my own eyes. Bits of objects do not disappear when there is nothing to make them disappear.

However, there is something which could produce these effects in apparently empty space and that is a very strong magnetic field. It is no good getting a magnet, shining light past it and hoping it will bend the light. The magnetism of all available magnets is far too weak for that. But what if we could produce the same level of magnetism as the UFOs emanate? Then things would be different – very, very different. The kind of magnetism that UFOs produce close to them is so strong that it can bend light vastly more efficiently than the best glass we can make. To understand this we are going to have to talk about the refractive index.

Refractive Index

A transparent substance's ability to bend light is given by a number called its refractive index. The values for glass lie between $3/2$ and 2 and that for water is $4/3$. What these figures really tell us is by how much a transparent medium slows the light that passes through it. The higher the figure, the more the light is slowed down in the medium and the more it will bend light that crosses it at an angle. To calculate the speed, turn the above figures upside down. For example, a really highly refractive glass will slow the light to half $(1/2)$ of its normal speed of 300 million metres per second and water will slow it to three-quarters $(3/4)$ of its normal speed. Of normal everyday materials, good glass slows light the most, but magnetism can, if strong, make the speed of light fall by a factor of ten or more – vastly greater than the best glass available. The fact that a medium has a refractive index tells us that the medium bends light which passes across its boundaries. The higher the index figure, the more capable of diverting light beams it becomes.

When Magnetism Bends Light

I came to understand the remarkable effect that very strong magnetism – what I call gigamagnetism – has on light rays in a strange way. At this time I did not often get a chance to read the science magazine *Nature*, but back in April 1961, when I was first researching this theory, I happened to come across a paper by an American professor, Thomas Erber, which suddenly gave me the means of calculating the effects that a UFO's magnetism would have on light. Erber (1961) deduced what happened to e-p pairs in a vacuum when magnetic lines of force threaded them and came up with a formula which gave the refractive index once you knew the strength of the magnetic field. The formula also involved the frequency of the light and made the refractive index

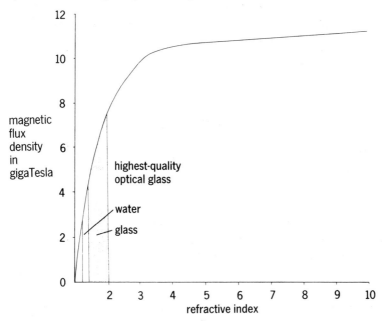

Fig. 8.2 When we plot the results of Professor Erber's formula, we find that if a UFO generates a magnetic field of about 3 gigateslas (GT), it will wallow in a refractive space with the same attributes to bend light as water. Increase the field to 8–10 GT and the vacuum will refract like glass. Above 10 GT the values of the refractive index shoot off to levels we are quite unaccustomed to. No one has ever experienced large volumes which can bend light so strongly.

higher the higher the frequency. Thus the effect on gamma rays would be higher than on ordinary visible light. Even so, with the giga-fields I was calculating, light was going to be highly affected by the invisible magnetic 'case' surrounding the hull of a UFO.

When I worked out the way the refractive index of empty space would vary with the giga-fields and plotted it (Fig. 8.2), I was astonished to find that, while the fields required were very strong, once you had achieved those fields you did not have to increase them very much before the refractive index shot off to incredibly high values – values much greater than anything we are used to in ordinary everyday refraction. The consequences of that discovery were startling.

Mirrors without Glass

Before we can appreciate the possible impact of Professor Erber's theory on our perception of UFOs, we will have to take the consequences of refraction a stage further.

Ordinary mirrors are silvered on the back of glass and therefore, whenever we look in a mirror, we get two images – one from the mirror surface at the back and the other from reflection in the front surface of the glass. This tends to fuzz the image. For ordinary home use, that is immaterial, but when it comes to optical devices like telescopes and binoculars, it becomes an unacceptable nuisance.

To overcome this we use either mirrors that are silvered on the front face or a property of glass which is called 'total-internal-reflection' (TIR). In prism binoculars, the distance the light has to travel from the front (objective) lens to the eye lens is increased by reflecting it several times, not in mirrors but in prisms. This increases the magnification, because the latter depends on how far the light has to travel between the objective and the eye lens. One way this is done is shown in Fig. 8.3.

Here so-called Porro prisms take light from the objective lens, reflect it at face A of one of the prisms, whose angles are 45 and 90 degrees, then in faces B, C and D and so to your eye, via an eye lens. There is no silvering on these faces; the light just reflects through a right angle every time it contacts the back of the apparently transparent glass. This is the rather remarkable

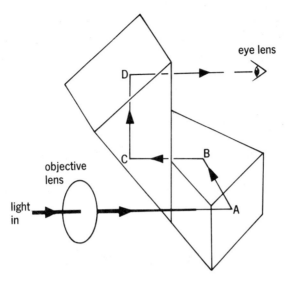

Fig. 8.3 How total internal reflection (TIR) is used in prism binoculars to increase the magnification by increasing the length of path the light has to travel.

phenomenon of TIR. But the effect can occur only when the light is in the glass and is moving towards the air. The same effect can occur in water or any other refracting medium.

Fish's-eye View

We are not used to being in a refracting medium and looking out into the air, but if you swim under calm water, turn over and look up you will find that your window on to the world above is a bright circular one set in darker surroundings. The surface of the pool has to be still for the best effect, but if you can do this you will know what it is like to be a fish.

A fish's view of the world is restricted to a circular patch in the water surface that subtends about 100 degrees at its eyes (Fig. 8.4). This is because, when the angle becomes greater than 50 degrees to the straight-up direction, the light comes from the bottom of the water, having been reflected in the surface by TIR. The light in the circular patch comes from the bank, the trees, the sky – whatever is above the water – but it will be a very distorted view of the real world. This angle of just less than 50 degrees is called the 'critical angle' and it becomes smaller the more refractive the medium becomes. For glass, it is about 42 degrees and as long as light meets a glass face from its inside at an angle greater than this, it will be reflected. This is why a 45-degree prism is such a useful device for binoculars, telescopes, etc., and as a bonus the TIR leads to almost perfect reflection, with none of the loss of brightness you get with a conventional mirror.

It does not matter how the refractive effect is achieved, but it is important to realize that the angles at which TIR can be achieved in the magnetic aura surrounding saucers may be very small indeed – only a few degrees – and must vary as the strength of the magnetic aura varies. If the saucer should surround itself with a magnetically stressed cloak which has a refractive index of 10 (as opposed to glass's value of 1.5–2), then the critical angle is only about 6 degrees. Increase the magnetism to give a value of 20 and it is less than 3 degrees. We see from Fig. 8.2 that once you have achieved a value of refractive index greater than 4, the sky should be the limit. It probably is not, but certainly once the magnetism exceeds a particular value small increases in the magnetic aura of

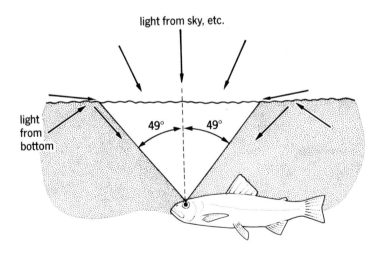

Fig. 8.4 A fish's-eye view of the outside world is restricted to a distorted image gathered through a circular patch which subtends just less than 100 degrees at its eye.

the saucer will stress its surroundings to make it wallow in a super-dense optical medium whose effects we need to investigate, as they way well explain some otherwise inexplicable observations made by credible witnesses. It might even explain how saucers can make themselves invisible.

One effect of the magnetic cloak about a saucer can be to cut down dramatically the amount of light coming from it. The gigamagnetic field about the saucer's surface will form a TIR 'mirror', reflecting much of the light either back into the saucer itself or on to the TIR mirror on the far side of the craft. Eventually some of this bouncing light will get to you, but it will distort the image you are seeing. When much of the light a UFO is producing is reflected back into itself it will produce a very dark-looking UFO. In other cases it will make for a very fuzzy image of what is, inside, a very solid object. The final effect may well be a round object, but one with very indistinct edges, and it may not be at all the same size as the original.

Here we see a reason why so many UFO pictures are indistinct and apparently out of focus. Stephen Darbishire's picture of the Adamski-type saucer (see Photo 15) was possibly thought to be out of focus simply because of this effect. Adamski's own pictures were sharp, because when he took them the craft was not surrounded by a very strong magnetic field. It was, in fact, just free-wheeling. However, when Jerrold Baker took his picture, the craft was in rapid flight and this could account for the blurring.

What refraction can do to the image we see of UFOs will be covered in the next chapter.

CHAPTER
9

Ghostly Images

BACK IN 1963 it was my privilege to entertain to lunch a fourteen-year-old schoolboy who had just taken one of the most curious flying-saucer photographs of all times. That boy was Alexander Birch, who, accompanied by his father, had come down from his home in Mosborough, Sheffield, Yorkshire, to be guest of honour at a LUFORO convention.

I have several of the original copies of the picture he took in 1962 with his simple camera and it is reproduced as Photo 1. There was no hint of a hoax. Alex was as honest as the day is long and his family was amazed by all the fuss, as was Alex himself. The local chemist who developed the roll of film did not at first print the famous picture, because he thought it was a 'spoil'. However, to researchers in the UFO field like us, it was an exciting thing to have what had to be a genuine photograph of not one but five flying saucers in formation.

We concluded, I think rightly, that if Alex was going to fake a flying-saucer picture he could never have made it so complex. In addition, there was the enigma of the 'space bubbles'. In front of and within the formation, there were groups of what were apparently bubbles. They looked a bit like soap bubbles, but were not independent of one another.

Basil Nubell, ARCA, LUFORO's photographic expert, analysed the picture, looking for spacial relationships between the objects on the photo. He found that the distribution of the images was not random. By imposing a square grid on the picture, he discovered a rigid parallelism between the positions of the objects, assuming that the picture is a front elevation, as seems most probable. As Nubell (1962) wrote: 'The lines of the module connect or relate edge and centre both horizontally and vertically.' Thus, he concluded, all five were images of the same object but the upper one was probably real and the others were 'radiation images' (what is meant by 'radiation images' will be discussed later). If you look at the four images, then, as we descend each one is a truncated version of the one higher up.

Then there are the 'space bubbles', which were arranged in five groups of three on arcs of circles or in straight lines. They acted just like transparent bubbles would do, because, according to Alex and his friends (whom he was trying to photograph at the time), they floated up and disappeared. They also refracted light, just as transparent bubbles would do.

Nubell was not the only photographic expert to examine the picture, and it was concluded that whatever the objects were, they were external to the camera – i.e. they were not emulsion defects; they were not implanted on the negative after processing; nor were they any form of flare-spot phenomenon. Alex's picture was pronounced genuine by a number of competent people (*LUFORO*, 1962a).

I met Alex again on Tuesday, 17 September 1963, in Studio 9 of the TV company Associated Rediffusion. The programme we were making was in their *Here and Now* series. The producer of this programme actually tried to be objective about a phenomenon which was being held up to ridicule by all the official sources. I was there to describe our Leviathan experience in Essex (see Chapter 2). During that short programme, the anchorman, Hugh Thomas, looked Alex straight in the eye and said, 'Now, Alex, do you promise that you didn't make all this up.' Without a moment's hesitation, Alex solemnly replied, 'I promise.' One needs to remember this when it is revealed that later, when he was grown up, Alex went on record as saying that the whole thing was a hoax.

The reason for this later denial was given by his mother in a letter she wrote to me early in 1966, because she felt she needed to describe to a sympathetic person the several close encounters Alex and his friends had had after the photographic event. Just as in so many other child-contact cases, the UFOnauts did not let the matter rest and one of the later visitations so frightened Alex that he decided he wanted nothing more to do with UFOs.

Mrs Birch described a UFO they had seen the previous November. It was, she said, 'A red ball glowing low down on the horizon. It moved fast, turning gradually, then stopped dead. Then it changed its shape until it looked like an hour-glass, then changed again and this went on for fifteen minutes.' She went on to describe the wealth of UFO events they had witnessed since Alex took the photo, concluding,

> Then there was this glowing thing that came on the ground just after a ray of light came from the sky. As the end of the ray had seemed to rest in a field about 200 yd away, my curious children climbed to the top of the fence to see if anything was about. They noticed this luminous mass rolling about in a field. Then they started yelling and jumped down and ran into the house. I couldn't get them outside the door again that night. This happened about 6.30 one November evening in 1963. The thing had frightened them with the way it changed shape from a shapeless thing into a ball, then an oblong, all the while glowing blue at the rim, with a pulsating yellow light in the centre. They ran because it came nearer and the way it moved sent young David Brownlow's hair on end. Alex heard a humming in his head and I'm afraid he will have nothing more to do with the subject or anything connected with UFOs.

It appears to me, having now read some of the wealth of literature on the contact cases, that the photograph was merely an opening gambit in a planned series of more intimate contacts, but because the boys involved were not prepared to co-operate, the attempts at contact faded. However, the humming in the head that Alex experienced has, in other cases, been associated with a certain level of programming so that the recipient can be contacted again if and when required. However, it need not have been anything more than an effect of the ultrasonic emanations from the 'skin' of the UFO (see page 106).

As if to corroborate Alex's photograph, a very similar picture was taken some four years later by a fifteen-year-old boy, Stephen Pratt (Photo 2). It was taken on 28 March 1966 at Conisborough, which is some 14 miles north-east of Sheffield. A bright light was seen by Stephen and his mother moving slowly across the sky. Stephen took one photo of the light, but when the picture was developed there were three dark UFOs, again in a rather rigid geometric configuration and with the same set of truncated images as in Alex Birch's photo. The middle and smallest ones seem to be possible radiation images of the largest one, also as in Alex's photo.

Radiation Images

How could a saucer reproduce images of itself in the space about it – assuming that that is what happened? Say we imagine that the magnetic aura of the saucer acts by TIR as if an invisible curved mirror exists behind it. That is how I first envisaged it and so I set out to see if I could reproduce Stephen Pratt's picture, using a torch bulb and a curved mirror. The bulb represented the light emitted by the UFO and the mirror its highly reflective, curved magnetic aura.

The set-up was like that shown in Fig. 9.1 (a) and when I photographed the results I was surprised at how like the Pratt and Birch photos the results were. Photo 3 looks wonderfully like three UFOs in formation, although only the middle one is real and the flanking ones are reflections of it in the mirror. How the images are formed in the mirror is shown in Fig. 9.1 (b), while the way the saucer might have formed them is shown in (c).

My laboratory experiment results are not quite the same as what appears in the Pratt picture (Photo 2), because in the latter it seems most likely that the left-hand image (1) is the 'real' UFO and (2) is a reflected image of that, while (3) is a secondary reflection of (2). However, the shape and distribution of the reflecting aura are unknown to us and will certainly be more complex than that of a simple curved mirror. There is also the possibility that none of these is a 'real' UFO and they are all projections in the aura due to another device. We cannot be sure, but certainly the idea of reflecting one image in a curved mirror, which is something that the magnetic-aura idea allows for, takes us some way along the road to understanding a phenomenon that would otherwise be quite incomprehensible.

I moved the camera a little and, to my surprise, got a picture (Photo 4) somewhat like Alex Birch's photograph (Photo 1). Because the mirror is curved and we are looking at it from just one point, the flanking images are truncated versions of the one in the middle – which is just how they appear on the photographs.

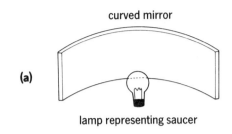

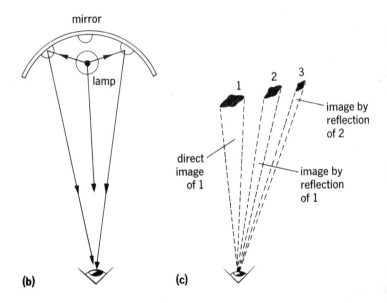

Fig. 9.1 **(a)** The simple laboratory set-up used to obtain Photos 3 and 4. **(b)** How the eye can see three lights in the direction of the mirror. In this case, the centre one is the lamp and the flanking ones are reflections. **(c)** Similarly reflections in the magnetic aura produced by a UFO can account for, in this case, the Pratt photo and, as in Photo 4, the Birch picture.

The one in the lower right-hand corner is a flare in the camera.

I am fully aware of the fact that if we are dealing with those who can manipulate the matter-antimatter 'sea' that fills all space, there is the possibility that they could work a piece of space to produce formations like the Birch and Pratt photos. However, the magnetic-aura theory is certainly one way it could have happened

1. The picture that Alex Birch took in June 1962 at Mosborough, Derbyshire.

2. A picture, similar in many ways to Alex Birch's, taken by Stephen Pratt in March 1966 at Conisborough, Yorkshire.

3. When a small bulb is reflected in a curved mirror, the result is very similar to the Pratt picture.

4. Moving the camera somewhat produces a picture that resembles the Birch photo.

5. An example of what an intense reflection can be produced in a refracting medium – in this case, a giant soap bubble.

6. The Army test the Charlton Hole for radioactivity in July 1963
(*Sunday Express*).

7. The photo that started a wave of interest in the crop-design phenomenon. These three circles were formed at the Punch Bowl, Cheesefoot Head, Hampshire in late July 1981. Never having before seen such circles at close range, Pat Delgado said that the impact on him was sensational (*Pat Delgado*).

8. The Mandelbrot crop design near Ickleton the day after its formation (*Cambridge Newspapers*).

9. The crop dumb-bell at Fordham Place, near Colchester, Essex, from the south.

10. The typical way that the stalks are swirled by the force sweeping the design. This is the south circle at Fordham again.

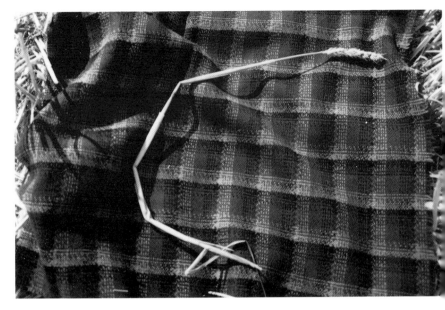

11. One of the wheat stalks from close to the central hole of the south circle at Fordham, showing the way it has been bent to follow the small radius.

12. The Reedlands Farm crop circles and triangle. The trails through the crop were made by us, the researchers, plus TV crews, etc. When these were first formed, the field was virgin apart from the tractor lanes (*Ron West*).

13. One of the larger 'canvases' produced by Mavis Burrows which shows Leviathan and what can only be technological constructions, communication antennae, etc. Writing appears in an unknown language.

14. Another of Mavis Burrow's drawings, which may include a representation of a 'vaid', plus a 'feather' design reminiscent of Hopi art and crescents like one that appeared in a crop design in 1992. The dotted lines seem to indicate communication channels.

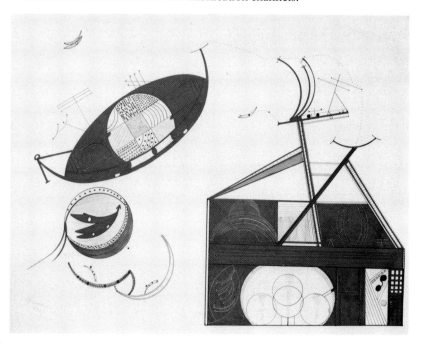

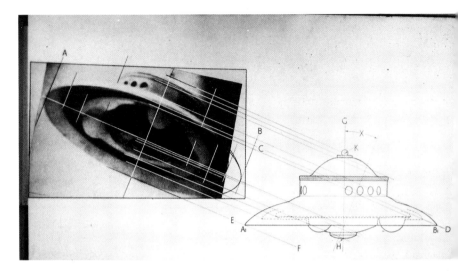

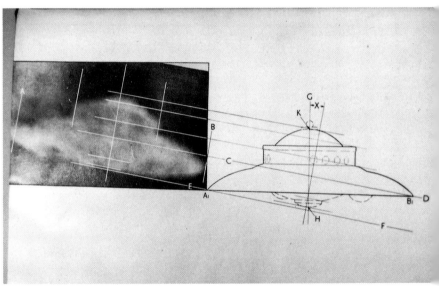

15. What is evidence? Photographs taken in California through a telescope (upper) and by a boy in Lancashire with a simple camera prove to be the same sort of object (from *Space, Gravity and the Flying Saucer* by L. Cramp). See also Fig. 4.4.

and it stems directly from the electromagnetic propulsion system I am envisaging.

If you doubt the ability of an invisible refracting medium to produce such reflections, look at Photo 5. It is Christmas morning and the author has given his young daughter a scientific toy for Christmas. It consists of a large plastic tray, some bubble liquid and a plastic ring that is about 1 ft across. With this you can make giant soap bubbles, and here is one of them floating ghost-like above the frosty garden. Everyone knows how thin is the film of liquid that forms a soap bubble and yet look at the bright reflections that have appeared in it. The dark castle-like image across the middle is actually two: one reflected in the front and the other in the back surface and so upside down. You can see two suns glinting past the edge of the images of the house, one upside down from the other. Then there are other secondary images of the sun in other parts as a result of internal reflections. And all of this is produced in a very thin shell of stuff which has a slightly different refractive index from its surroundings. Yet you can see the bird-table and the trees through the bubble.

Such an example of refraction may help to explain strange reports like the following (Good, 1992). On 15 August 1990 two people at Babinda in Queensland, Australia, saw a bright moon-sized object. It was oval in shape and hovered in the night sky, exhibiting a set of smaller lights around its circumference. Although the object was brightly lit, the witnesses said they could see the stars through it. No noise was heard and the sighting lasted three minutes. As you cannot see through the bodies of real UFOs, this observation must have been, partially at least, of an image that was being projected in some way akin to the method outlined above.

Such observations as these, which are too strange to be made up, illustrate the fact that UFOs can do all kinds of things to the light that emanates from them using strong magnetic fields. These effects may be a natural accompaniment to the saucer's propulsion system or they might conceivably be produced for a special purpose. Here is how shape-shifting, so beloved of fantasy writers, could become a reality. You need only the right sort of gigamagnetic aura and the shape of anything can be apparently changed to something else. Note, however, that the emphasis is on 'apparently'. With flying saucers, seeing may not be believing. In fact, if and when you see a UFO, and the UFO researcher comes to call, describe carefully exactly what you saw, but just keep in your mind that you might not have been seeing the real thing.

Strange Disappearances

One of the things that astounds observers of certain UFOs is their apparently ability to suddenly disappear. One moment the UFO is there and the next it has gone. For example, Sharon Robbins describes a UFO sighting she had at midnight on Sunday, 15 May 1977, in the so-called 'Welsh Triangle' (Paget, 1979). The area covers that furthest extremity of south-west Wales around St David's Head, where an incredible set of UFO-related events occurred in 1977 and 1978. Sharon was driving home when she saw a large 'ball of fire' hovering close to the brow of a nearby hill. It was lifting and sinking and twice she thought it landed. After the second landing, this large white light floated across a field. To her it seemed as large as the moon. She said, 'When it reached the other side of the field, which was still within eyesight, it vanished. The light didn't fade at all, it just disappeared. The whole thing lasted for about five minutes.'

Another apparent 'disappearance' was reported from St Mary's Loch, Selkirk, Scotland, in August 1990. One Saturday morning at about 8 a.m. an artist, John Hay, saw a totally silent, pale, greenish-grey object flying over his isolated house. It was shaped something like a rugby ball, with pointed ends and stubby wings in the middle on either side. Together with his son, he watched the craft, which they estimated was about 400 ft up and travelling at about 70 m.p.h. Hay himself temporarily lost interest, but his son continued to watch the strange craft. On being momentarily distracted by his father, the boy glanced away, and when he looked back the object had literally disappeared. Both were adamant that it could not have been lost behind the hills that surrounded the loch.

To show it is possible for such things to happen, we can do another very simple experiment, which anyone in a school or college physics laboratory can emulate (Fig. 9.2). It is best to use a laser beam, because the latter is so strongly defined and you can

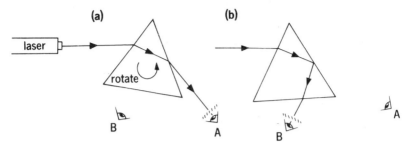

Fig. 9.2 A laboratory experiment with a laser beam and a prism. **(a)** With the prism in this position, A can see the beam, but B cannot. **(b)** A slight change in the refracting medium (the prism) leads to A suddenly losing the image, while B gains it. Again, it is TIR that is responsible.

see at once what is happening to the light. Put an equilateral prism (one with 60-degree angles) in its path and shine the laser beam on one face at a fairly large angle (a). Someone at A (wearing protective goggles) views the beam coming out of the opposite face of the prism. Now slowly rotate the prism, making the angle at which the light enters the prism smaller. At a certain angle, the beam will suddenly disappear, but someone else at B will be able to see it reflected by TIR on the inside of the face of the prism. In other words, as far as A is concerned, the beam has vanished. The person at B knows where it has gone, because he or she is looking at the prism from a different angle and can see the path of the beam inside it, but say there was no prism to be seen. Say the beam came from a UFO which suddenly turned on its propulsion system and by so doing shot its light off, away from you to somewhere else. You don't know where it has gone and for you the light from the craft has switched off, even though in reality it is shining as brightly as ever.

This simple experiment with one beam illustrates what can happen when we begin to deal with UFOs and their gigamagnetic fields. And there is another everyday illustration of not believing what you see.

On hot days roads often look 'wet' and the reason is that a layer of hot air exists over the road surface. As in Fig. 9.3, the light that comes to you from the road surface is actually light from the sky which has been refracted. You can sometimes see trees and buildings on your horizon mirrored in the surface. But

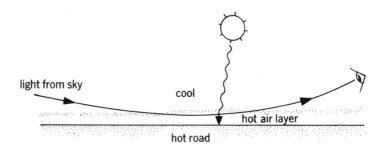

Fig. 9.3 How a hot layer of air produces a reflection of the sky that makes the road look 'wet'.

why 'wet'? The answer is that a layer of water lying on the road will, by a different method, also produce a reflection of the light from the sky. The wet road is more familiar, so when we also see sky light in the road on hot days, we compare it to wetness, knowing full well that we are being deceived.

One consistent observation of both Leviathans at altitude and saucers at close quarters is that they reflect light like polished metal. When metal is polished you put a minutely thin, flat layer on its surface which acts much more like a mirror than the previously grainy unpolished metal. In the case of the magnetic aura about saucers (and, one assumes, Leviathans), the effect like the 'wet' road surface occurs just outside the skin of the device. This means that however dull or otherwise the real surface is, it will always make sunlight, or other light, glint from it in the way that polished metal does.

Projecting the Effects

It seems that sometimes UFOs are able to project this ability to bend light. One of the most bizarre cases concerned an Australian businessman, Ronald Sullivan, who on the night of 4 April 1966 was driving from Wycheproof to Maryborough, about 100 miles from Melbourne (Lorentzen, 1966). It was a moonlit night, but the only adequate illumination was from his own headlamps. Suddenly his headlamp beams bent to the right. Sullivan, who at first instinctively followed them, managed to avoid the ditch and the fence as he swiftly brought the car to a halt.

The bent beams struck a cone-shaped object standing in a field. It was a column of light about 25 ft high, 3 ft wide at the bottom and 10 ft wide at the top. The bottom appeared to be on the ground and was a brilliant white, but the rest was a cloud-like mass emitting all the colours of the rainbow. Before the astonished driver could make any further move, the object rose silently and vanished at tremendous speed into the sky. The headlamps were now functioning normally, but even so he had them checked when he got to Maryborough just to make sure.

There was a sinister sequel to this event, for three nights later, when it was overcast and pitch black on this straight piece of road, nineteen-year-old Gary Taylor was found dead in his car at the same spot. He had run off the road. Police checking for clues found a circular impression 5 ft across and a few inches deep in the freshly ploughed field next to the road. There seems to be a definite possibility that this same object had been the cause of Taylor's death, as he instinctively followed his headlights in the darkness (Lorentzen, 1966).

Here we have a very bright UFO showing all the signs of a gigamagnetic field about it. For instance, it was fuzzy because the parts of the aura that emitted visible light were diffuse and not at all clearly defined. They also varied, leading to the many colours. At the bottom, the force field was so strong that it emitted only a brilliant white. It was also a curious shape. UFOs that are thin and tall like this are rarely reported. The actual shape could not, of course, be seen within the radiating aura, but it must have had a physical base which was 5 ft in diameter. This made the visible aura twice the physical size at the bottom and suggests that the object was shaped like a miniature steeple. It seems likely that the magnetic radiation that was enough to bend Sullivan's lights was projected in some way from the craft, because the normal magnetic aura would not have been strong enough to bend the headlamp beams in the way they did.

Another case which illustrates that UFOs can affect the ignition of vehicles at a considerable distance occurred near Fordingbridge, a town on the edge of the New Forest in Hampshire. It was 2.30 a.m. on 6 November 1967 when Karl Barlow came round a bend in his truck and noticed a bright object above the trees on his right. It was approaching him and was, he estimated, about a quarter of a mile away when the radio and lights of his vehicle went dead. The diesel engine, however, continued to function as normal.

With no lights and with the craft descending to the road about 45 ft ahead of him, Barlow brought his truck to a halt. He sat amazed as a sort of trap door opened in the bottom of the craft and a kind of 'vacuum cleaner' device began to suck up grass, gravel and dead leaves from the side of the road. It then moved to the other side of the road and did the same thing. Then, after hovering for about thirty seconds, the object took off and returned from where it came.

Barlow said it was about 15 ft in width and generally 'egg-shaped', but it was an 'out of this world' green. He also had a witness. The driver of a white Jaguar car coming the other way suffered failure of his engine, as well as his lights. In both cases the batteries of the two vehicles were found to be dead (Lorentzen, 1966).

So here we have further proof that vehicles without electric ignition do not suffer engine failure in the electromagnetic aura of UFOs. In at least one other similar case the battery has boiled, which could be the result of the alternating magnetic field forcing a large alternating current in the battery. This would heat up the electrolyte and so lead to the battery boiling. We have to realize that the detailed effects are different in each case, but even so, evidence certainly seems to point to a large alternating magnetic field surrounding UFOs and so leads us back to large electric currents in the surfaces of the UFOs. Which means we can, with more confidence, seek the reasons why such devices can at most times make no noise, while at others produce terrifyingly loud noises. This we will do in the next chapter.

CHAPTER 10

Sounds from Another World

THE SOUNDS AND SHOCK WAVES experienced at and around Warminster in 1964–5, some of which were described in Chapter 2, give only a glimpse of the ordeal suffered by the people of that UFO-stricken place.

For example, Eric Payne was walking home from Sutton Veny – a village 4 miles south-east of Warminster – at 11 p.m. on 28 March 1965. There had been a heavy snowfall, which had now been followed by fog. He was close to Drayton's School at Bishopstrow when he heard a whistling noise that developed into a loud buzzing. At first he could not make out, through the thickening fog, where this strange noise was coming from. He was soon left in no doubt, though, because almost immediately some form of flying object passed over him, flattening tree-tops on either side of the road and making a tremendous racket. He described it as sounding like a gigantic tin in which huge nuts and bolts were being rattled about. He then experienced great pressure on his head and neck, just as Marjorie Bye had done the previous Christmas morning. At the same time, something seemed to sting his hands and cheeks, while a strong wind tore through his hair and burnt his eyes. His head rang with the whining waves of sound and his eardrums seemed to be near bursting point.

Between the paroxysms of having his head rocked from side to side and the complete immobilization of his arms and legs, Eric Payne managed to get a glimpse of 'the thing', which he described as a pale shadow that was shaped 'like an oval dish'.

Unable to rise against the burgeoning pressure, he crawled around in the road, eventually sinking into the soaking wet grass of the verge. As well as being held down in a vice-like grip, he also had to undergo the ordeal of feeling the skin on the back of his neck contract and turn to ice. Yet, at the start of the experience, he had felt heat and a prickling sensation like needles digging into his flesh.

Just as with so many other people who have had lonely but close UFO encounters, he could not at first tell anyone about the experience. It was some days later that he confided in his parents, but while the mental scars might remain, he apparently suffered no long-term physiological effects.

John Cleary-Baker, one-time editor of the *BUFORA Journal*, investigated the Warminster sounds and concluded that two distinctly different effects had been reported.

One is a sound like innumerable stones colliding, 'resembling maize or gravel being tipped on to a concrete surface'. This is interspersed with sharper cracklings, like 'atmospherics' on the radio.

The other sound is a persistent humming which 'rises to an intolerable and high-pitched whining as the UFO passes over the auditor'.

It is important to notice that the 'gravel' noise has a low frequency, while that of the humming is very high – maybe rising into ultrasonic realms. The gravel noise was said not to change much, but the humming rose in pitch as the UFO approached. This was maybe the same effect we get when police-car and ambulance sirens approach – the pitch of the already ghastly noise increases.

Supersonic Sound Waves

Here we see two new effects from UFOs – ones which are particularly associated with the Warminster flap, although not exclusively so. Now we have to seek some effect of the aura of UFOs that has a new physical dimension. We need to move up several orders of magnitude from EM effects in our search for a possible explanation of these 'savage sound waves'. We must leave the world of electronics and go to the world of the pressure waves we call sound.

The science of magnetohydrodynamics (MHD) describes

what happens to magnetic lines of force when they interact with ionized clouds of particles (plasmas). In the diagrams that help explain the theory, arrows (vectors) indicating magnetic fields, forces, electric currents, etc. stick out in many directions, because the whole interaction is three-dimensional and difficult to visualize. However, for us there is an important simplifying idea.

Imagine the magnetic lines of force as stretched elastic strings which repel one another when they crowd together. If we apply the idea to force arms rotating round the surfaces of a saucer, a model would have the magnetic lines represented by rubber bands stretched round a cardboard strip shaped as in Fig. 10.1 and placed over a force arm (a).

That is how they would look when rotating slowly, but speed up the rotation and immediately the bands would tend to get left behind, as if friction with the space over the saucer surface were holding them back (b). The faster the rotation, the more the bands will be left behind. Eventually they become so stretched

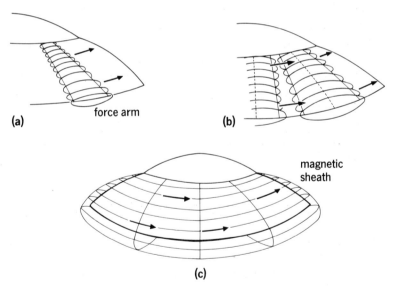

Fig. 10.1 (a) As a force arm has an electric current flowing in it, the magnetic lines of force can be thought of as elastic bands round the force arm. **(b)** As the force arm gathers speed, the magnetic 'bands' become stretched and may overlap. **(c)** Eventually, when the rotation rate is high enough, the saucer becomes covered in a high-density magnetic sheath.

that they overlap the next force arm and then the effect is as if a continuous sheet of rubber were stretched over the surface (c).

This elastic sheet will be in tension and so, just like the skin of a drum, it oscillates with a natural frequency which depends on how tightly it is stretched. Interestingly, seeing the number of observers who report humming sounds, this frequency could, under some circumstances, be close to the '50-cycle hum' we hear from the transformers of electricity substations. This would apply to a saucer the size of Adamski's – i.e. about 10 metres in diameter.

Because the elastic sheet of magnetism is stretched, it stores energy and would make the magnetic effects near the saucer surface even stronger than those described in Chapter 7. Increasing the rotation rate as the saucer builds power also compresses the sheet into the saucer surface and makes the whole magnetic skin very stretched, very dense in magnetic energy, and increases the natural vibration frequency.

Now the saucer begins to act somewhat like a strangely shaped organ pipe and it resonates at frequencies we can expect to hear, as well as many which will be above our natural range (Fig. 10.2). We can work out what the frequency will be when we know the size of the cavity in which it occurs (like the length of the organ pipe) and what is known as the Alfven velocity. The Alfven velocity can be found once we know the strength of the magnetic field, and making a few valid assumptions we conclude that the 10-metre-diameter saucer could generate sounds around 100 hertz (cycles per second) – i.e. twice the 50-cycle hum from electrical appliances. These would occur where the magnetic field strength was quite low; increase it and the frequency of the vibrations will sing up through the high octaves and out into the ultrasonic range, above our ability to hear. However, that will not prevent the eardrums trying to respond to these unnaturally high frequencies made at unnaturally high intensities. The result would be the feeling that the eardrums were ready to split.

Nasty Sound Effects

It is well known that the most disastrous of low-frequency sound (infrasound) is 7 hertz. This frequency has been investigated as a possible weapon of war, to be beamed at the enemy and so lead to disorientation, nausea and trauma, making it impossible to fight. It also produced the same symptoms in the scientists making the experiments and nothing more has been heard of the idea. However, it illustrates that should a UFO produce such vibrations, the effect on a human being would be catastrophic.

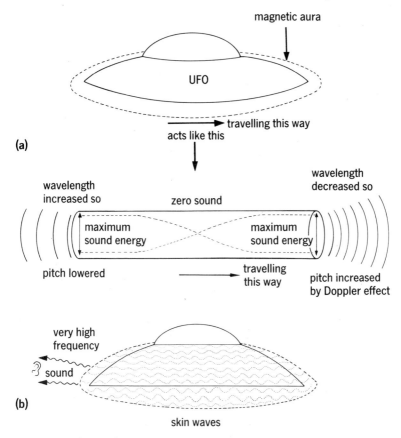

Fig. 10.2 (a) The 'organ-pipe' analogy to explain the way the magnetic aura acts to produce an intense, relatively low-frequency vibration which communicates itself to the air and so to unfortunate observers. When the 'pipe' moves towards the observer, the sound pitch increases by the Doppler effect, while it correspondingly goes down in pitch as the saucer moves away. **(b)** The high-frequency 'skin' waves in the surface of the magnetic sheath produce a sound of much higher pitch, which may indeed be in the ultrasonic range.

The theory of MHD waves suggests that a large UFO (say 300 ft across) could generate such a frequency when its magnetic field was low.

Other Waves

As well as the long waves generated by the whole of the magnetically stretched space about the saucer, there is going to be another set rippling across the surface of its magnetic membrane. It is the difference between bouncing on a trampoline and hitting it somewhere with a mallet. To make it more akin to what we are describing, the normal canvas sheet would need to be replaced by a thick rubber one attached rigidly to the frame. Bouncing will make the rubber sheet vibrate slowly in time with the bounces, while the mallet will send out small waves through the 'skin' of the trampoline. In the case of the MHD cavity surrounding the saucer, we will call these 'skin waves'. So we have two possible sources that could link with the air and send 'savage sound waves' to the unfortunate person who was close to the saucer. This is roughly what Cleary-Baker concluded from interviewing the witnesses.

The Shock Front

When a supersonic aircraft approaches the speed of sound (which is about 300 metres per second), it must expand the air, but the air will only dissipate the energy at its natural speed – i.e. the speed of sound. So as the plane accelerates through the sound barrier, the air cannot transmit the energy fast enough and it builds up an almost solid wall of air along surfaces called shock fronts. These shock fronts are the V-shaped ones seen streaming back from the nose, etc. on drawings of supersonic aircraft to illustrate their ability to travel faster than sound (see Fig. 7.2). It is the passage of the shock front that creates the sudden assault on our eardrums which is the 'sonic bang'.

Anything that tries to make sound travel faster than its natural speed will create shock fronts and the magnetic sheath around a saucer will do that. This is because the Alfven waves created by the magnetic shell have a speed which adds to the normal speed of sound and so supersonic waves are broadcast from the saucer surface. However, this creates a shock front surrounding the craft. This boundary to the shock waves will be something like 100–150 metres from the surface creating it when the UFO is generating giga-fields and becomes closer as the field drops in strength. Anyone subjected to a UFO the shock front of which is close to the ground will experience what amounts to a continuous sonic bang. At Warminster, for reasons best known to themselves, the UFOnauts sent their craft over at a height where the horizontal sheets of shock waves were able to strike birds, roofs and people.

Electromagnetic Wind

Because of the way I think it is propelled, the UFO must also ionize some of the air around it. Calculations show that we do not need a very strong field and nor do we need to ionize the air very much to create a wind of 30 knots which will blow back and forth in sympathy with the rotations of the force arms. This may be the wind which Eric Payne (and also Ronald Wildman, see page 52) saw buffeting the tree-tops as their low-flying UFOs came close. There is, however, another possibility: that the magnetism itself interacting with the sap in the branches, etc. might be able to create the effect of a violently turbulent wind. Ideas about that will have to wait for Chapter 14.

Certain brave or foolhardy people have experienced some of these effects when approaching UFOs on the ground. One such was James Flynn, who on 12 March 1965 went into the Everglades in Florida with the intention of doing some hunting. Because three of his four dogs had managed to get lost, he decided at about 1 a.m. to go and try to find them. Riding his swamp buggy in the direction the dogs had gone, he was diverted by a brilliant light which, after some jinking about, seemed to be descending. He ran it to earth through some cypress groves and, getting quite near to the object, saw that it was a huge disc-shaped craft with four tiers of black-edged lights encircling it. These light patches, which he described as 'windows', were about 2 ft square and the bottom tier started about 12 ft above the base of the object, while the top tier was about 8 ft below its top. He estimated it was some 70 ft across and half that high. The patches gave off a pale yellow light, while an orange-red glow illuminated the ground below the UFO.

Apparently undismayed by this great device, Flynn decided to go closer. He was now aware of a sound like 'big transformers' that increased as he approached the object. Abandoning his buggy, he walked up to the edge of the thing and was then aware of an anticlockwise swirling wind that was coming from below the saucer. It was strong and akin to the prop-wash from a plane. Flynn waved to try to contact the occupants, but all he got for his trouble was a 'short white beam of light' that hit him between the eyes so that he lost consciousness. An Indian friend rescued him, but he was unconscious for a full twenty-four hours, and even after a month was still feeling the effects. Checking later, it was found that there were freshly burnt and scorched tree-tops in the area, as well as damage consistent with a large object having scraped down the sides of the trees (Lorentzen, 1966).

So here we have something like the '50-cycle hum', which Flynn only experienced when he got within the compass of the shock front but which grew more intense as he got closer. We also have a wind that is being entrained by the idling force arms. Flynn may have thought that he was 'attacked' by the UFO, but in reality he may have been saved to hunt another day, because approaching close to UFOs is a very foolhardy thing to do. If the UFO had decided to take off, he could have been badly injured or even killed by the strength of the force field about the saucer.

Back to Warminster

That the Warminster sounds are described as alarming is not at all surprising. Here is a form of noise unlike anything ever heard before. We cannot yet create the massive volumes of strong magnetism that give rise to the MHD waves and so no one in a laboratory has ever experienced the effects they will create. When they do, they may well look back at the testimony of the stricken people of Warminster and see that there was something scientifically important that should have been investigated, if only they had not been so frightened of jeopardizing their positions in the scientific hierarchy. One cannot help wondering whether maybe

Warminster was not chosen by some of the UFO denizens as a test laboratory for their own experiments. Certainly the experiences of people there seem to be unique, in the sheer intensity with which they occurred if not in the actual events.

Even so, when the 'savage sound waves' kill a flock of pigeons in flight we are dealing with something that has not been reported that way before – or since. This macabre event occurred at Crockerton near the Longleat estate in Wiltshire in February 1965, where the pigeons tumbled out of the sky into a woodland clearing. Gamekeepers also found pheasants dead in peculiar circumstances, and some caged birds as well, after a visitation from 'the thing'. Yet it was not only birds that suffered. Mice were found burnt and riddled with small holes in the garden of a house which had been sound-blasted.

No Sonic Bang?

It is often remarked by sceptics that UFOs cannot be real because they accelerate to vast speeds way above the speed of sound and yet they do not make a sonic bang. Anything, they say, that is solid and speeds up to, or slows down from, thousands of miles an hour must announce its presence with the bang.

That would indeed be so if the surface of a saucer were its real boundary, but it is not. The saucer's surface of contact with the air is possibly yards outside it and it is not a sharp surface. Near this boundary ionized air will be entrained by the magnetism, separating the air so the UFO can slide through it. As it shoots off into the blue, it is throwing intelligence of its coming ahead of itself. It will part the air gently enough so that the latter does not exceed the critical speed of sound. It will thus ease through the sound barrier and there will be no sonic bang. The same applies as UFOs slow down from supersonic speeds.

In the next chapter we will explore how it is that people can get sunburnt or, even worse, be actually burnt by observing UFOs.

CHAPTER 11

The Radiation Aura

IT WAS ABOUT 10.30 p.m. on Sunday, 26 October 1958, when two men only identified as Messrs C and S were taking a car ride near Loch Raven Dam, which lies north of Baltimore, Maryland. By so doing they came within a few hundred feet of a 'large, flat, sort of egg-shaped object which was hovering about 100 ft above the superstructure of Bridge Number One. This bridge is not visible until you take a left-hand bend beyond the dam itself and then it suddenly comes into view.'

Mr C is quoted (Vallée, 1967) as saying:

We slowed and then decided to go closer and investigate the object. We crept closer to the object along the road leading to the bridge. When we got to within 75 to 80 ft of the bridge the car went completely dead on us. It seemed as though the electrical system was affected; the dash lights went out, the headlights went out, the motor went dead. Mr S, who was driving the car, put on his brakes and turned the ignition once or twice. We didn't get any whirring sound. We were pretty frightened at this point. We both got out of the car. On this road there is nowhere to hide or run, which is probably what we would have done. So we got the car between the object and ourselves. We watched it from that position for approximately thirty to forty seconds and then – I am not sure of the sequence of events here – it seemed to flash a brilliant white light and we both felt heat on our faces. Concurrently there was a loud noise that I interpreted as a dull explosion and Mr S heard as a thunder clap. Then very quickly the object started to rise vertically. It didn't change its position as far as we could tell during the rising. The only different feature it had while it was moving was that it was very bright and the edges became diffused so that we could not make out the shape as it rose. It took from five to ten seconds to disappear from view completely.

Mr S independently verified this statement, saying that when the electrics failed it was like 'someone had taken the battery out of the car'. He estimated the object was about 100 ft long and said that it was glowing with an 'iridescent glow' before the blinding light appeared, and the wave of heat seemed to be 'something like an ultraviolet light or some kind of radiation'.

After the object had gone they found the car worked perfectly, but next day both of them had slightly reddened faces as if they had been sunburnt.

So here we have some form of radiation spreading from the UFO as it gathers power which is accompanied by the equivalent of a sonic bang. I think the bang was when the magnetic shock wave passed the observers and, as it was heat, was intense infrared light. However, as the craft generally brightened at the same time, both visible and ultraviolet were also present. That the aura surrounding the craft made it fuzzy, whereas before, when it was just hovering, it had been more or less sharp, backs up the ideas outlined in previous chapters.

The experiences of the Baker family (Landsbury, 1976) illustrate many of the facets of the radiation auras of saucers. The account is long and only some of it can be paraphrased here. On the evening of 13 March 1975, at about 9 p.m., Philip Baker, a machine operator of Mellen, Wisconsin, was alerted when his badly frightened daughter ran into the house and said that there was a UFO sitting on the road. He described it as dome-shaped with a brilliant halo. Bluish-green lights and red lights were round the outside and in the centre it had a brilliant yellowish-white light that appeared to be coming from inside (translucent?). It was so bright that he said he had to squint to look at it.

The object was making a loud, high-pitched whining noise. Baker's family had joined him to look at the object and as they watched the high-pitched noise died away. 'It was,' said Baker, 'as if it ran down.' The coloured lights dimmed then went out completely. The halo that covered it dimmed considerably and then the UFO made a noise like 'heavy metal hammering' but without a rhythm. Eventually the aura also completely disappeared, there was a bang and the object had gone.

About forty-five minutes later UFOs were observed in the neighbouring area of Iron County and George Ree, the undersheriff of Mellen, was again called out to look into the matter. Among the UFOs seen was one which to Ree, at a low level, was flashing a green and white light. To his colleagues, observing it from a tower on a hill, it was blue and white. Ree was very troubled by this difference in observed colour and asked himself if he was colourblind. He need not have worried, because if the light was synchrotron radiation, then it could look blue from one elevation and green from another, just as observed.

We have here the high-frequency sound which can be formed by magnetic skin waves. Later we get the lower-frequency resonant noise, due to vibrations of the magnetic cavity in which the UFO exists. In the end we get the 'sonic bang' as the shock front sweeps across the Baker family. Also we see the way the light dims as the skin-wave noise also dies away, showing they are linked to the same basic cause – i.e. the running down of the power, which means that the gigamagnetic field is much reduced and the synchrotron radiation must fade out. Only the ionization light remains and eventually even that goes. At that moment the UFO must have been almost inert. This is, however, just prior to switching on full power, when the shock front was generated and the object disappeared into its own cloak of magnetic invisibility.

Translucent Saucers

The idea that synchrotron radiation is a major source of the light from UFOs means that the visible light will come from a layer that lies above the UFO's surfaces but will not actually be on the surface. It is like sheathing the UFO in a blanket of light. From the layers inside the blanket will come the higher-energy radiations, like ultraviolet, X-rays and gamma rays. From layers outside we will find invisible heat radiations being given off. The UFO's ability to contain its own radiation will act most strongly on the higher-energy radiations, but the light and heat will be broadcast more intensely.

Here we see why people describe UFOs as being translucent. Stephen Darbishire, struggling to describe the way the Adamski-type saucer he saw looked, said that it had a silvery, glassy appearance, 'like metal or plastic, which light goes through but which you cannot see through' – a good description of translucence, in fact.

A piece of ground glass is translucent because most light is coming from its back surface. This is just what happens when a 'blanket' of light covers a saucer. The brightest light will come from the inside of the blanket and will be predominantly blue-violet. It will shine through layers where the colours that are emitted are those of the rainbow, culminating in red on the outside. Vary the intensity of the magnetic field around the saucer and these colours will change, maybe producing the 'all the colours of the rainbow' effect seen by Ronald Sullivan in the bent-beams case (see page 100).

However, in general the surface of the saucer people see will not be its real surface, because the 'blanket' from which the light is coming lies some distance above the real surface (Fig. 11.1). Because of this, it is possible to think you see the bell surface of a saucer rotating when in fact it is only the blanket which is rotating. This makes sense of the observations of UFOs the bell surfaces of which appear to rotate while the cupola remains

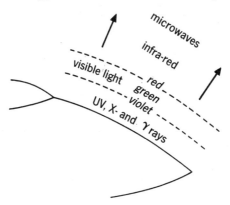

Fig. 11.1 Because synchrotron radiation becomes longer in wavelength as the magnetic field strength lessens, the surfaces producing it are covered in layers from which different rays emanate. This could produce the translucent effect so often reported and means that the surface seen is not necessarily the actual surface.

stationary. Of course, in actual fact the whole craft is stationary and only its aura is rotating.

Means of Heating

Infra-red and ultraviolet radiations are not the only means by which UFOs can produce heat. In fact, they may not be the most potent ones. That accolade belongs to something already mentioned in the previous chapter – namely, ultrasonics. In this we have to include microwaves, because here only frequency matters and although these two may be different physically, they occupy the same frequency range. Thus they can produce the same devastating effects on those unfortunate enough to be subject to them.

The ultrasonic waves will stem from the 'ripples' in the surface of the magnetic shell and need air to carry them. The microwaves will be generated by synchrotron radiation in an outer blanket some way above the UFO surface and, being EM waves, will not need air and will, for example, be able to penetrate into the cockpits and cabins of high-flying aircraft.

Noon on 1 July 1954 saw the start of a sequence of events which ended in tragedy. An F94 Starfire fighter was scrambled to intercept what the pilot could soon see was a gleaming disc-shaped machine. As he started to close in, a 'furnace-like' heat filled both cockpits of the two-seater. Through the blur of heat the pilot jettisoned the canopy and saw the radar-observer bale out. Stunned by the experience he was undergoing, without thinking the pilot also baled out. Clear of the cockpit he immediately came to and was horrified to see the plane crashing into the town of Walesville, New York State. Four people died in the ensuing inferno, while several others were injured.

Because of the cover-up the aircrew, already going through hell, were sworn to secrecy by the US Air Force, who spread it abroad that it was merely engine failure that had made the men jump. It was fourteen years before the truth was told, and then the pilot described a secondary effect which made his mind black out, so that he did not even remember bailing out. He recalled the heat and the observer bailing out, but nothing more until his parachute opened.

Keyhoe (1957) says:

Several investigators believe this case indicates that the aliens are not hostile. No attempt was made to injure the pilots after they bailed out. Apparently the heat force was used only to keep them from closing in to attack. There are several other cases which appear to reinforce this opinion.

A similar event was described by Carlos Alejo Rodriguez, a pilot and parachute instructor of the Uruguayan Air Force (Keyhoe, 1957). Flying near Curbelo Naval Air Base he encountered a domed UFO about 70 ft in diameter. It came towards him, then stopped and hovered, so Rodriguez decided to risk a closer look. Half-way to the disc, he was almost suffocated by a wave of heat. As he hastily banked to escape, the UFO sped away and the temperature returned to normal.

Now, maybe Keyhoe was right and the heat 'attacks' were deliberate attempts to stop the jets closing in. But there is another interpretation. Did the pilots simply fly into the zone of the UFOs' aura, which occurs naturally, and when clear of the aura there was no further effect? Or can the natural aura be controlled and directed to produce such results? To answer these questions more research is needed, and maybe only governmental agencies world-wide have sufficient information to reach a sensible conclusion.

The Theories of Dr Fontes

Dr Olavo T. Fontes became a major investigator of UFO events in Brazil in the 1950s and was the Brazilian representative to the prestigious American UFO study group APRO. Fontes was one of the first to authenticate the notion that waves of UFO sightings occurred at recurrent intervals and could therefore be predicted. He detected a twenty-six month and a five-year cycle which enabled him successfully to predict waves in the late 1950s and the 1960s. He also, incidentally, confirmed my observation of the five-year recurrence of Leviathan sightings in my own area (reported in Chapter 3). Unfortunately, Dr Fontes died at the age of forty-three on 9 May 1968, so it is now impossible to know whether he might also have narrowed down his five-year waves to the arrival of Leviathan expeditions over the same parts of the world at intervals of exactly five tropical years.

However, the theories of Dr Fontes on the origin of heat waves from UFOs are what most concern us here. They came as the result of the so-called 'attack' on the Brazilian Army garrison at Itaipu in November 1957.

Two sentries on the ramparts of the Itaipu fort spotted a bright-orange light coming in from the sea. It was dark and the soldiers' curiosity turned to fear when the light grew larger and larger until it stood some 300 ft above the fortress.

Suddenly, a strange humming noise was heard and an intense heat enveloped the two men. One collapsed, while the other managed to crawl to shelter behind a nearby cannon mount, screaming a warning to the rest of the garrison. Later the sentries said that they felt that their clothes were on fire and the heat was suffocating.

About a minute later the lights of the fort went out. Despite the ensuing panic in the dark, the emergency generator was started but immediately failed. By the time the others had gained the ramparts, the UFO was on its way back out to sea.

When the two men were admitted to hospital a strange thing was discovered. Although they both had second- and third-degree burns over large parts of their bodies, the burns were only in areas *covered by clothing*.

Fontes correctly concluded that only one physical effect could have produced such burns: ultrasonics – what Fontes termed 'structural heating'. All sound waves, whether ultrasonic or not, are longitudinal. This means that the vibrations of the particles occur in the direction of travel of the sound waves. Electro-magnetic waves are transverse in that the vibrations of the particles which carry the wave energy are perpendicular to the direction of travel. In this they are like sea waves, where the water molecules vibrate up and down as the waves pass. Sound is unique in the way the molecules move forwards and backwards in response to its energy.

However, ultrasonic waves are converted from longitudinal to transverse whenever they meet a layer which is essentially different from that next to it. A good example is between clothes and skin. Here the transverse waves are more readily absorbed and lead to heat being generated along the interfaces. This is exactly what happened to the unfortunate soldiers at Itaipu and here we have another example of the possible effect of the MHD skin waves.

From his researches, Fontes seemed to think that the ultrasonic 'weapon' was a short-range one, which would fit well with our ideas of the air being set into vibration by the ripples on the magnetic skin. In the Itaipu case it seems that the ultrasonics were able to burn the sentries before the magnetic aura was able to nullify the electrics of the fort, which would be in accordance with our theory.

Fontes also pointed out that ultrasonic vibrations bypass the ear and act directly on the brain. He imagined that the UFO denizens had perfected a means of modulating the ultrasonic waves so that they could 'play on the organism the way a musician plays on his instrument – creating emotional moods that strike too deeply for an untrained animal to resist. Dogs would be especially sensitive' (Lorentzen, 1966). This insight could be the explanation for the way animals are petrified by the proximity of UFOs – seemingly more than humans. However, noises, etc. produced 'in the head' without going through the ear are often reported by those who have close contact encounters with UFOs. Often the result is a feeling of well-being or even amnesia. What gives credence to Fontes's suggestion is the number of people who suffer some kind of cerebral disturbance after the initial event, often for a long time.

So, it was almost certainly ultrasonic heating in the case of the Itaipu sentries, but whether the UFO meant to produce that effect is doubtful. Or maybe it did not care about the effect it had on two soldiers and just did what it wanted to do. After all, it did not kill the men; it only burnt them somewhat. If the UFO had been commanded by people with the thought processes of humans and who had an awesome power at their command, would those sentries have still been alive after the incident?

When jets are scrambled to try to shoot down UFOs, remarkably all that happens is the UFO responds with a little scientific wizardry designed to put the interceptors off. What happens afterwards is not the fault of the UFOs. They do not provoke attack and do not want to be attacked. When they are, they defend themselves with minimum force – which is more than can be said for the military authorities of the world.

CHAPTER 12

Beams That Probe and Create

ONE EVENING IN OCTOBER 1963 an Argentinian family was visited by a set of UFOs that used beams to 'investigate' buildings on their farm. They lived 2 miles north of Trancas, which is in the Tucuman province of northern Argentina. The Belgrano railway line runs past their farmhouse and, slightly nearer to the farmhouse, runs a road (Fig. 12.1).

The family had retired to bed early – about 8 p.m. – because their private power plant had broken down. Later, when it was dark, members of the family were awakened by strange lights that appeared to be on the railway line. They first noticed two separate bright lights a short distance apart, which were joined by a tube of light in which the silhouettes of human-like figures moved. On venturing to the farm gate, which faced the railway, some of the family became aware of a green light close by in front of them. Thinking that it might in some way be connected with one of their farm vehicles, they shone a torch on it, whereupon six glowing 'portholes' opened up round a 30-ft-wide and 10-ft-high saucer-shaped craft. The UFO, which had a dome on top, was floating some 5 feet off the ground and was a mere 15 ft away from them (Fig. 12.2).

As they watched, the portholes began to change colour in rotation and what they described as a 'burst of flame' sent them reeling and fleeing back to the safety of the house. Those left in the house watched the saucer apparently rotating as it became enveloped in a white mist, which quickly changed to orange. A 'tube of light' then emerged from the top of the saucer and played on various parts of the house. Eventually they were dismayed to discover there were three UFOs, around and close to the house, together with the two by the railway line. As well as the tubular white light from the UFO mentioned above, one of the others sent a similar but reddish-violet beam towards the farm. Two of these beams played on a shed housing a tractor and one of the farmer's married daughters, Yolie, went as far as to thrust her arm into one of the nearest beams, which she described as being like 'a glowing liquid'. The beam generated heat in Yolie's arm and this alarmed her, so she ran back into the house. As the beams investigated other buildings, as well as the farmhouse itself, the temperature in the latter rose from a mere 16°C (61°F) to a sweltering 40°C (104°F). At the same time, the interior of the house was as bright as day.

Then, abruptly, the phenomenon came to an end. The saucers near the house switched their beams away from the farm and all five objects assembled on the railway line, moved off and were not seen again.

Yolie's description of the tubes of light looking like a liquid indicates that just as liquid has a higher refractive index than air, so the tubes must also have had a higher refractive index than their surroundings. Yolie could see the edges of a beam so clearly that she was able to thrust her arm into it. She probably wanted to see what it was made of. When her arm began to get hot, she decided that discretion was the better part of valour and escaped into the house, but this is not the ordinary light you might get from a searchlight.

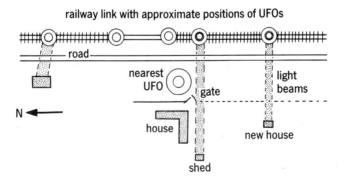

Fig. 12.1 Sketch of the Argentinian farm.

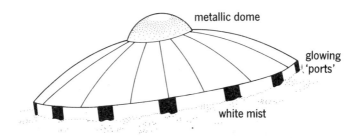

Fig. 12.2 Eyewitness's sketch of the UFO that was close to the gate.

The effect is well known to science: it occurs whenever a very strong beam of EM radiation passes through the air. Most people will have seen this in laser light shows; the effect of the intense EM waves in the beam compared to the space through which it flows is to make a change of refractive index between the beam edge and its surroundings. This, with the help of motes of dust in the atmosphere, makes the beam much more sharply defined than one would have expected. The sharp liquid-like edges of the beams that probed the Trancas farm were therefore beams of intense EM radiation, but they were not ordinary beams of visible light. A major constitutent of the beams was probably microwaves, which means that the adventurous Yolie could have had a cooked arm had she not withdrawn it when she felt the first hint of heat.

We cannot, of course, be sure what the total constituents of the beam were. However, they were, almost certainly in this case, electromagnetic and not ultrasonic. There were no reports of hummings in the head or similar manifestations. What happened here was that beams which co-operated together were able to penetrate solid buildings and create EM effects within them. They could create light within the room without doing so outside, and the same went for heat. They could well have been receiving back in the saucers on the railway line a complete kind of three-dimensional representation of, say, the tractor in the shed, as well as the interior effects and the occupants of the house. The beams could have produced a complete interior surveillance of the farm without the need ever to enter any part of it. We can understand a way in which this could happen through holography.

Lasers and Holography

Holography, meaning the whole image, is a relatively new science on earth but will be old-hat to the UFO denizens. We can give instances of visions that have been witnessed in the past which were thought of then as paranormal but are now recognized as possibly holographic images. We will give some examples later, but for now it will be helpful to explore holography first.

The reason why holograms have had to wait so long for explanation after the nature of light was understood is that you have to have very well-ordered light to create them. At the moment, only the laser can create what is called 'coherent' light and even then the coherence of lasers is not perfect.

The word 'coherent' has the same connotations as in ordinary speech. If you are coherent you put words in the right order and the right context. Lasers put light waves in order before they broadcast them, and in this they are unlike light bulbs and fluorescent tubes, which broadcast light that is hopelessly jumbled up. The eye does not care that the light is jumbled, so we do not suffer any loss of vision because of it. However, it makes the bulbs and tubes very inefficient and costs us all a great deal of money in wasted electric power. Minute beams of coherent laser light contain more usable energy than wide beams of ordinary light, simply because the immensely large number of individual packets of light (photons) which make up the beam are coming out of the laser with their waves vibrating in step with one another. It is this property of photons vibrating in synchronization with their fellows that makes the light coherent.

On the other hand, the photons in, say, the beam of a torch are in step with their fellows only by sheer chance. We can make them more coherent by forcing them to go through narrow slits or small holes, but then we lose most of the energy of the light. So at present the laser is king in the business of making coherent light, and the important property of coherent light is that it can produce interference effects very efficiently.

We can see the effects of interference simply by overlapping two parts of a plain net curtain and moving them about. For the best effect you want to be looking at one of the yellow (sodium) street lamps but, in any case, you will see changing patterns of dark and light generated by the interference of the two sets of threads and holes. The threads represent the troughs of light waves and the holes the peaks. Where troughs and peaks coincide, there will be a dark band. Where hole and hole coincide there will be a bright band. These patterns of dark and light bands, when produced by light waves overlapping one another, is what is called interference of light. However, interference can occur in any kind of waves. For instance, in the ocean, when sea waves and swell waves combine, it makes trains of waves, some of which are bigger and some smaller than average.

To produce interference patterns, we need two coherent beams of light, and the best way of getting that is to take one beam and split it into two. Then let the two partial beams travel different paths and recombine them somewhere else.

However, if we split a laser beam (Fig. 12.3) and make one half-beam play on objects such as, say, chesspieces, the chesspieces will reflect the beam (a). If we make that reflected light interfere at a photographic film with the other half-beam, which goes straight to the film, the result is a pattern of dark and light areas which contain the information about the shape and relative positions of the chesspieces in three dimensions. Pass the same laser light through the negative, which is now a hologram, and view the result from the far side but at an angle (b). You will see a three-dimensional image of the original chesspieces. You can move your eye about and find that, just as in real life, a chesspiece in front of another moves in relative motion with the one behind.

Holograms can be created in full colour by using different kinds of laser, so were the white and reddish beams from the UFOs at the Argentinian farm coherent laserlights, able to intefere with one another and so create heat and light within the house, but, because they were modulated in a certain way, only in the house? Did the interference of the beams as they fell on objects in the house produce a kind of three-dimensional feedback signal that could be picked up and recorded by the UFOs, so giving them a picture of what and who was in the building? When UFOs project beams on to objects, buildings, etc. on the ground, is this what they are doing? Not looking *for* something but looking *at* something of interest to them?

Thus they may well already know where the gold lays stashed away in the vaults of Fort Knox and how much there is. In fact, one of the most talked about encounters between a terrestrial aircraft and a UFO occurred over Fort Knox. It was the fatal encounter on 7 January 1948 between Thomas F. Mantell's P-51 Mustang fighter and a saucer which Mantell described as 'metallic and of tremendous size'. The story appears in many early UFO books, as in those days no one knew whether the saucers were friendly or hostile. The fact that Mantell's plane was found 'literally torn apart and that the residue looked like kindling wood' (Lorentzen, 1966) was taken as a sign that the

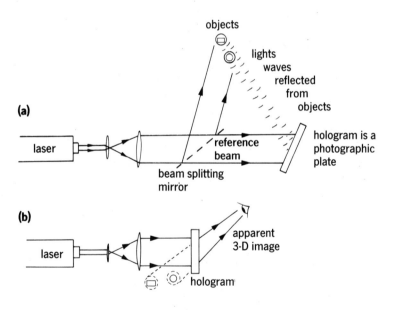

Fig. 12.3 How a hologram is made. **(a)** The narrow beam of the laser is broadened and passed through a mirror that lets half the light through and reflects the rest. Light wavelets reflected from the objects interfere with the direct reference beam and store the information about them on the plate. The result is a hologram. **(b)** Now put the hologram back in the same beam, view it as shown and an apparent three-dimensional image of the objects is obtained. Move your eye and the objects move in relative motion, just as in real life.

UFOs were hostile, but after the millions of UFO sorties flown since then in the skies of the world, such an idea is, I believe, untenable. If the UFOs, with their devastating abilities to repel unwanted attentions, had wished to be hostile to us, then we would have already have had a 'War of the Worlds' scenario visited upon us. In fact, the exact opposite has happened. The levels of UFO activity may have waxed and waned over the years, but the UFO denizens steadfastly refuse to make direct contact. The Mantell tragedy was, I believe, an accident and one which the UFOnauts would like to have avoided, because it spawned the 'scramble and chase' phase of US policy and effectively precluded any chances of meaningful contact there might have been. We now realize that the space races are doing things differently. They appear to be infiltrating our species through individuals, who they often imprint as children and contact through the rest of their lives (Strieber, 1987).

Victorian Close Encounter

One of the best descriptions of the use of holography by space denizens comes not from the modern era at all but from 1871. On 4/5 October of that year a much respected and competent builder, cabinet-maker and undertaker of High Wycombe in Buckinghamshire had an encounter with robot-like devices which he was constrained to discover in a wood near his home. Nothing would have been known of this encounter had not the amazed William Robert Loosley, then aged thirty-four, committed a long account of the encounter to paper and tucked it away in a drawer, fearing the obvious ridicule and loss of credibility that attempted disclosure to the close-knit Victorian community would have provoked. His account is so remarkable that it has to be as true as he could make it. The full account is given by an honours physicist David Langford, who provides an edited version of Loosley's many pages (1979), as well as a highly incisive commentary on what was shown to Loosley in holographic images during the encounter.

Briefly, in the early morning of 4 October Loosley felt he needed to get some air and so left his house. He witnessed, as a result, the 'fall of a star', which became brighter than the full moon and was accompanied by a noise like thunder which apparently only he heard. It came to rest and sank into a clearing in a copse on Plummer's Hill, in full view of his house and south of Hughenden Manor, the then home of Benjamin Disraeli, for whom Loosley did some work.

Later that day, intensely intrigued by what he had seen, he set his apprentices to work and walked out to the wood to look for traces of the overnight visitation. What he found – or maybe what found him – was a metallic robot about 18 in tall, covered in flat plates on which were various protuberances. The object first uncovered a glass or crystal lens about 1 in across and then produced what we might today describe as a photo-flash of violet light from another similar opening. It then extended a pointed arm at him and retreated into the wood with Loosley following. Curiously, rather than fear, he felt pity for the alien thing that he concluded was lost in the wood.

He saw it extend an arm with a claw on it and lift some small dead rodent from the undergrowth. It proceeded to wrap the prize in a plastic shroud and deposit it inside itself. Soon he and the robot were in the central clearing and Loosely detected what he originally expected to find: the foliage had been pressed down over a wide, circular expanse.

The small robot proceeded to herd Loosley across the clearing and then revealed a larger one hiding in the undergrowth. The small robot transferred its wrapped rodent to its larger brother, which twinkled with small lights.

Then started what today we would recognize as a holographic show. First, he was shown himself, but when he tried to touch himself his hand went straight through the image. The larger object was projecting the images, while the smaller 'stood guard' behind Loosley.

The bemused man was treated to a counting session in which he was given some basic mathematical sequences of numbers shown by flarings of the holographic image. He was given the numbers of the Pascal triangle, which connects to a universal mathematical pattern that, like the periodic table of the elements, would be recognized by anyone in the universe (Fig. 12.4). Then he got the sequence 1,1,2,3,5,8 . . . which are the first six terms of the Fibonacci series, in which adding the previous two numbers gives the next. Here, as the numbers increase, the ratio of any succeeding pair comes closer and closer to the mystical golden ratio of 1.618. This 'magic' number is denoted by the Greek letter *phi*, and among many other properties it gives the proportions of the Pyramid of Cheops at Gizeh, near Cairo, in their simplest form – i.e. base; apothem; height as 2; *phi*; root *phi* (Fig. 12.5). The human body is also constructed in conformity with this ratio.

These universal truths (the word math is, I believe, one and the same as Maat, the name of the Egyptian god of truth) may have been to establish that the originators of the show had the same rational, logical minds as earthly mathematicians. Although all this was lost on the practically-minded Loosley, some form of imprinting must have occurred, as the man remembered so well a sequence of events so alien to his level of knowledge.

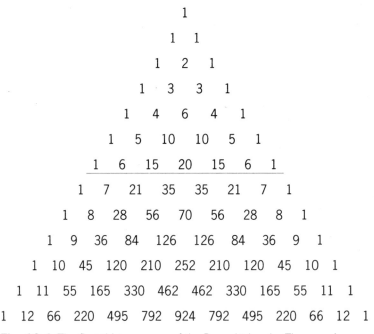

Fig. 12.4 The first thirteen rows of the Pascal triangle. The row shown to Loosley is underlined and is the seventh row from the top. For the mathematically-minded, these are the coefficients of the expansion of $(x + y)^6$.

(a)

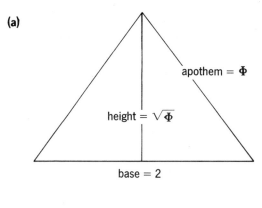

apothem = Φ

height = $\sqrt{\Phi}$

base = 2

(b)

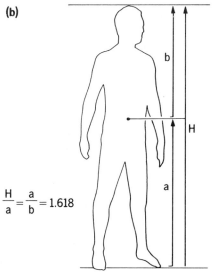

b

H

a

$$\frac{H}{a} = \frac{a}{b} = 1.618$$

(c)   1, 1, 2, 3, 5, 8, 13, 21, 34, 55, etc.

$$\frac{55}{34} = 1.6176 \simeq 1.618 = \Phi$$

Fig. 12.5 (a) The proportions of the Great Pyramid are most easily expressed in terms of the golden number *phi* (1.618). **(b)** The normal human body has proportions based on the golden section, which yields the golden number. **(c)** The first ten terms of the Fibonacci series as shown to Loosley. Each term is the sum of the two before it and any term divided by the one before it will, as the number grow larger, yield a number closer and closer to 1.618.

As the experience progressed he was shown the planetary orbits of the solar system and maybe those of the planet from which the devices came, but, most amazingly, his description of what follows can be interpreted only in the light of the probability distribution of the atom. The images described can only be those of the so-called s and p orbitals, in which the electron is most likely to be found. They may have gone further, but Loosley had difficulty in describing even these images, whose basis would not be revealed to the world of science for another fifty or sixty years.

It must be realized that when Loosley was shown these wonders the electron was not even established as a particle (1897), quantum theory was not formulated (1900) and the nucleus was not even suspected. The first real theory of the atom did not emerge until Niels Bohr formulated it in 1913, at a time when Einstein had not published his theories of relativity. Bohr, however, managed to find only the key that unlocked the atomic secrets; Max Planck had, some years previously, discovered the bases of quantum theory. So even a top physicist would have

Fig. 12.6 The symbols that were revealed to Ludovico Granchi in July 1988. Compare those of Figs. 4.2 and 4.3.

found it impossible to make any sense of what an untrained cabinet-maker was given. It would appear that the whole exercise was designed to be recorded, as Loosley obediently did, so that one day, when our physics had advanced sufficiently, it could be found and we would know that 'they', while more advanced than us, had travelled the same tortuous path to knowledge.

Move on 120 years and holographic presentations are still being made. At 4 a.m. on 31 July 1988 a UFO stopped over the house of Ludovico Granchi, who lives at Itacunuca near Rio de Janeiro. He estimated (Bartholomew, 1991) it was about 200 metres up. In his own words:

> It suddenly emitted a brightly lit white panel with writing in black letters on it. The borders of the panel were also black. On impulse I ran to fetch a pad and pen, and I started to copy down what I saw. This phase must have lasted for about ten minutes, during which time I did my best to copy faithfully what I was seeing, and as if guided by an invisible hand to take down the message. I cannot tell whether my copy was a faithful one. I was in a panic. It was a strange sensation.

Possibly Ludovico had been already marked, as he had had a UFO encounter as a young child and was 'taken back' for examination in September 1988. The recollections of the latter abduction involved humanoids who, he said, 'chirruped like crickets'. Thus it is likely that he was chosen to receive this message because of his previous experiences. Further, his mother is a Brazilian consultant to *Flying Saucer Review*. Thus once again the UFOnauts were pretty sure that their intervention would not induce hysteria in the one with whom they chose to communicate.

Just as in so many other cases, Ludovico did not comprehend anything of what he had written down (Fig. 12.6) and the writing looks like, and yet not like, the writing on Adamski's photo plate or in Homet's book (see Figs. 4.2 and 4.3). What are the communicators trying to tell us? Discussion of that knotty problem will have to wait until Chapter 14.

CHAPTER
13

Amazing Effects

THERE ARE some wonderfully strange things reported by competent observers when UFOs are around and because they are based on advances that we can hardly contemplate, they may well be dismissed as the wanderings of diseased minds. That does not, however, preclude their being true descriptions of what the witnesses saw.

One of these sightings took place among the forests and lakes of Finland in midwinter. It was Wednesday, 7 January 1970, and by 4.45 p.m. it was already dusk when forester Aarne Heinonen and farmer Eske Vilje were skiing their way homeward through a windless glade to the village of Imjarvi. Despite being in the south of the country, it was intensely cold: −17°C (close to zero F).

The two men had stopped to rest in the glade when they experienced a buzzing noise. They connected it to a brightly lit object flying in from the north. As the object circled in towards them from the south, they saw that it had a luminous red cloud rotating about it. The thing came down to about 50 ft and they could see that the cloud shrouded a circular metal object about 10 ft in diameter, with three hemispheres on the underside and a central tube projecting below the craft. This tube, they estimated, was about 1 ft in diameter.

Eventually the object came to within about 12 ft of the ground, whereupon the buzzing ceased and a patch of light was projected on to the snow from the central tube. This patch had a black edge to it and, as they watched, the black ring rose and shrank until it was a black disc small enough to disappear into the tube. This was followed by the descent of the red mist to the ground and then the light beam with its black edge reappeared. At this point, one of the two men experienced an involuntary sort of convulsion in that his head was jerked backwards. Then, to their astonishment, both of them saw a man-like creature appear in the light beam. Its face was waxen and it had a large hooked nose. It appeared to be dressed in greenish overalls, darker green boots to above the knees and white gauntlets. In one gauntlet this 3-ft-high figure held a small black box. The box had a hole in it, from which emerged a pulsating yellow light, while at the same time a whole shower of large sparks came from the dark circle on the snow.

As they watched, the apparition turned the box towards Heinonen and directed the yellow beam at him. The big sparks were also hitting the men, but they felt nothing. Then the red mist thickened and expanded out to envelop the two astounded observers. It became so dense that they could not even see each other, yet they were just able to pick out the light beam that was flickering like a dying flame as it disappeared back into its tube. The witnesses then said that the mist was 'thrown apart' and the UFO had disappeared. The whole episode lasted some three minutes.

Both men suffered effects from this encounter. Heinonen was numbed and at one point fell to the ground. He had to be helped home on foot without his skis by Vilje. He was off work for several months with headaches, sickness, backache and lethargy. Both he and Vilje had to be treated for shock and both developed swollen faces and had very sore eyes.

Now what do we make of all this? Charles Brown, editor of *Flying Saucer Review*, says, 'I wonder whether or not the Finns witnessed an illusory image projected in some incomprehensible way from the UFO?'

To me that seems the most likely explanation. Bowen describes the whole episode as particularly pointless, which to us, who do not know what its purpose was, is certainly true. It is obvious, however, that the UFO specifically picked these two men before delivering its illusion and, while we cannot hope to know what was behind the visitation, we can at least try to understand some aspects of it.

What intrigues me is: if the two men could have approached the dwarf and had tried to touch it, would it have had any real substance? In other words, was it another holographic image or did the projection possess a certain amount of solidity?

One clue may lie in the red mist, which was shrouding and moving round the craft. It was there before the dwarf appeared, absent when he manifested and there again when he disappeared. Despite their advancement, the UFO denizens cannot go against the basic laws of nature (the intelligence on maths and physics given to William Loosley back in 1871 shows that – Chapter 12). They may be able to manipulate those laws more subtly than we can, but they cannot create something out of nothing. Einstein's general relativity theory tells us that we cannot create matter without expending a great deal of energy, and even the UFOs may not have that level of energy at their command. However, the fact that the red mist was rotating shows that it must have been ionized or else the magnetic field of the UFO could not have entrained it.

Can We Have Molography?

For a long time I have dabbled with the idea that it should be possible to form a complex electromagnetic matrix and, with ionized molecules, form what I call a molographic image. This would be like a holograph but the illusion would be fleshed out with real matter. In other words, in the case of the dwarf, there would have been substance to him: he would have been made in three dimensions, not just of light apparent only to the eye, but of molecules sewn together in a pattern determined by interfering beams projected down from the UFO.

Thus I would define molography as the science of creating an electromagnetic grid of interlacing beams that can, when fed with ions, produce the shapes and attributes of real objects. The extra ingredient we must have over and above a holographic illusion is the ionized atoms or molecules that can be pulled in and arranged to coincide with the 'knots' of interference between the projected beams. Was that why the UFO brought a red mist with it, so that it had some material substance which could be used to form the body, clothes, black box with its light, etc.?

The mist became the dwarf and when the UFO switched off the show, this material expanded out to envelop the onlookers. If it was a mist of ions, was it a surfeit of ions that the two men suffered from for so long? That, together with the 'sunburn' from too close contact with the radiation aura of the device?

If, as in Fig. 13.1, the black ring had been connected with a magnetic mirror, then it would have appeared black to the onlookers. This is because it was reflecting EM waves only inwards towards the apparition, so leaving little light to be emitted towards them. Comparing this case to a holographic image, they could have had a reference beam and outside it a secondary beam, carrying the 'information' to create the dwarf that was reflected from the black ring. The high EM field needed to create the ring may have provided the necessary potential over a highly insulating snow-surface to produce electric sparks. Of course, we cannot be sure about any of these things, but that should not stop us speculating within our limited scientific knowledge.

Do we have here an example of a fairy – a word which, I often speculate, might come originally from 'of air'? Have the UFO denizens played these kinds of games with people in the past, forming images out 'of air' and giving shows to certain chosen people, often to children? Is it not a fact that even today many UFO manifestations are made to children? The photos taken by Stephen Darbishire, Alex Birch and Stephen Pratt are just a few of the examples. It is becoming increasingly obvious, as we study the phenomenon more deeply, that UFOs which make close contacts do so because they want to. There is a purpose, even if we do not divine that purpose. In years to come the advance of scientific knowledge may well reveal some of the purposes of the UFOs, which is why *all* the events ought to be recorded, not just those that appear to make sense.

It is a crime against our future understanding when self-professed UFO experts dismiss events that they cannot understand. They think they know what the UFO phenomenon is in all its aspects and on this flimsy basis 'evaluate' the testimony of witnesses. When they then state that the observation was of some everyday object like a weather balloon, they are often guilty of branding the observers at best as having mistaken the evidence of their own eyes and at worst as charlatans or hoaxers.

Possibly there has been more harm done to the cause of understanding UFOs by its more avid devotees than by all the powers-that-be in their campaign to debunk the whole phenomenon.

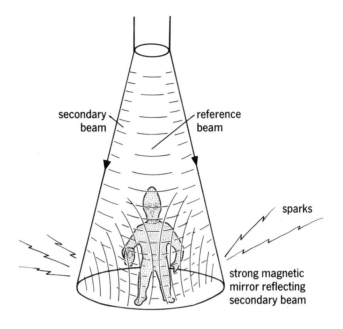

Fig. 13.1 An impression of the Finnish 'dwarf' and how it might have been produced as a form of 'molographic' image.

Whatever the answers, the experience of Heinonen and Vilje is one of those bizarre events which fuel the sceptics' criticism – and incidentally waste reams of print in useless consideration of matters which they do not understand.

Science can, however, shed some light on certain curious events that otherwise do not make much sense: for example, the Vashon Island (Washington) encounter on the night of 18 February 1968 (Lorentzen, 1969).

Three boys in their late teens, Richard Frombach, Boone Powers and Chris Beachner, had driven into an old gravel pit on the island. It was raining heavily when they observed a glowing object resting on a hill to the east of the access road they were on. The road ended in a pond. The boys described the object as oval or crescent-shaped and said it gave off a pale bluish glow (Cerenkov again?).

They were pretty convinced that what they were looking at was out-of-this-world and excitedly drove back into town to get some of their friends to come out and take a look. When they got back, the object was still there but had moved to the left of its original position. They now saw that it was about 30 ft in diameter. Possibly thinking there was safety in numbers, they once more drove back into town to see what other witnesses they could find.

When they returned the object had gone, but the pond, so recently water, was now frozen over. What staggered them was that it was not a cold night and there had not been a frost in the area for days. No other ice was to be found anywhere other than covering this pond.

On investigation, the ice was found to be formed in layers and was in places 5 in thick. It was also full of air bubbles, many of which contained dirt from the bottom of the pond. This latter fact is of extreme importance if we are to explain this apparently inexplicable happening. How can a pond freeze on a warm night? Maybe this way.

Boiling Water into Ice

One of the scientific 'tricks' I always enjoyed performing in my work as a physics lecturer started with my telling incredulous students that I was going to 'boil water into ice'. To do so, I put a little cold water from the tap into a test-tube and supported the arrangement under the bell-jar receiver of a vacuum system. I then proceeded to pump out the air from the bell jar.

As you do this, bubbles begin to rise from the bottom and sides of the test-tube and soon the water is boiling merrily – so much so that you have to have a strong drying agent in the jar to mop up the copious amounts of water vapour produced. The water sometimes boils so violently that it erupts out of the test-tube all over the inside of the bell jar. Eventually, however, the water goes quiet, because we have boiled out most of the air trapped in it.

Those who have not seen what happens to water under a vacuum are surprised that a thermometer I put in the tube at the start is reading just a few degrees above freezing! Soon they are even more surprised to see that a layer of ice has formed on the remaining water. This layer thickens with time and may get nearly half an inch thick before I stop the experiment.

The heat for this boiling lies latent in the water: the only thing that prevents water boiling at a temperature lower than the normal 100°C (38°F) is atmospheric pressure. Reduce that pressure and the minute air cavities in normal water expand and rise. As they expand on rising, they are full of water vapour, which erupts into the air as the bubbles burst at the surface.

Every gram of water vapour that escapes can do so only because of the heat it takes from the water. In fact, every gram of vapour takes away seven times the amount of heat that is required to freeze a gram of water into ice. So looked at this way, it is very easy to boil water into ice.

In the Everglades case (see page 109) James Flynn experienced a rotating 'wind' coming from below the saucer as it hovered. Where could such a wind be coming from? Certainly not fed down through the saucer. What the latter must have been doing is creating a vacuum below it by entraining the air and throwing it out to the sides. Now, assume that the 30-ft saucer the boys saw went and hovered close over the pond. It is certainly highly probable that it could also produce a vacuum and the pond would have boiled. We find dirt from the bottom in the bubbles, which is just what we need to find if the explanation is to hold water (excuse the pun!). It would naturally have got rid of the water vapour it produced by throwing it out sideways, so keeping the space under it 'dry' and allowing the boiling to have its head. Again, some of Flynn's health problems may have stemmed, like Heinonen's and Vilje's, from a surfeit of ionic wind.

Saucers as Vacuum Cleaners

In July 1963 a hole 3 ft deep and 5 in wide appeared in the line of division between a field of potatoes and a field of barley. Roy Blanchard, who farmed the land at the Wiltshire village of Charlton, not far from Shaftesbury, was astounded to see that without the slightest sign of anyone visiting the spot, there was not only this strange hole but also a circular depression surrounding it from which soil and plants had been removed, as if by some vast, circular vacuum cleaner.

Around the central hole – dubbed the Charlton Hole at the

time – was a shallow depression about 8 ft in diameter and about 3–4 in deep from which the potato plants had completely disappeared. Beyond the hole a very few plants remained out to about a radius of 12 ft. As well as the plants, some 1,000 lb of topsoil had gone missing, apparently sucked into the air and certainly never discovered elsewhere (Chapman, 1969).

When Blanchard scratched his head for an explanation, he could imagine only that an alien spacecraft had dropped into his fields overnight and 'harvested' his crops. The Army took a great interest in the Charlton Hole and tested it for radioactivity, but all they discovered were some ironstone rocks at the bottom of the hole (Photo 6). It would appear that the UFO which took the plants and the soil also took a 'core sample' as well, but it may also be that the hole was a necessary part of the process of providing enough energy to extract all that weight of earth.

As almost invariably happens, there were reports of UFO activity in the area at about the same time. In the early morning of 13 July Mr C. C. Palmer had stopped his car for a rest on the A30, not far from Shaftesbury. In the car were his brother-in-law and some friends and the former called attention to a light just below the rising moon. This happened to be roughly in the direction of Charlton. The light traversed the sky from south to north and they had it in view for a full five minutes while it changed direction several times. They heard no sound from the object they assumed was carrying the light, which appeared to have no definite pattern of flight. It eventually disappeared over the horizon behind a clump of trees. Whether this was Roy Blanchard's harvester or not we do not know, but it seems very likely. Maybe its wayward flight was because it was seeking the right crops and position for its night work.

The case for earth-gathering UFOs is further strengthened by sightings of it actually happening. In France in October 1954, a French farmer, M. Cazet, was startled to see a

> luminous body balancing itself lightly in the air, to the right of the plum tree as it prepared to land. As well as I could judge, this object was about 3 metres in diameter and seemed elongated, horizontal and orange-coloured. Its luminosity threw a pale light on the branches and leaves of the tree (Michel, 1954).

When the craft had gone, from where it had landed the earth had been 'sucked up' so that on the fresh soil of the hole 'white worms wriggled'. Just as with Roy Blanchard, to M. Cazet it seemed as if the clods of earth had been hauled out by a giant vacuum cleaner.

This ability to create a vacuum and extract earth – sometimes in large quantities – is not a necessary side-effect of the landing of UFOs. Many, indeed the vast majority, of UFO landings result only in some indentations where it is assumed that landing gear has rested and/or scorched earth or vegetation plus flattened grass, etc. None of these effects is the same as what gives rise to the present wave of designs drawn by invisible means in the growing crops of the world, but most particularly in the south of England. It is these and their ramifications that we will discuss in the next chapter.

CHAPTER 14

Hieroglyphics in the Corn

WHILE THE great waves of UFO visitations of previous decades have at the time of writing waned, the UFO denizens have found a new and unequivocal way of communicating with us. They have taken to drawing more and more complex patterns in our fields of standing corn. Here is something which cannot be wished away by the sceptics and the hoaxers have been very hard pressed to produce a copy of the real thing. In fact, the only hoax which has really confused the experts needed the discipline of the Army plus some 'spies' within the ranks of the circle-watchers (Good, 1992).

Circles of flattened corn have appeared for many years in corn fields in many areas and while they remained circles, certain meteorologists, in particular Dr Terence Meaden, were able to develop a more or less convincing theory that they were produced by vortices in the air. However, the phenomenon has since then become so complex in its manifestations that no one can any longer entertain the idea that a purely natural meteorological phenomenon is responsible.

It was Pat Delgado who, in 1982, alerted the press to the oddity of a circular formation in a field at Cheesefoot Head in Hampshire. There, totally divorced from any sign of human intervention, were three beautiful and precise circles in a line, the larger one set centrally between the two identical smaller ones. The centre circle, Delgado found, was 56 ft across, while the smaller ones were exactly half of that (Photo 7).

Within the circles the ripe corn had been gently laid over, each stem being bent at the point where it emerged from the ground, and all the stems were laid in a clockwise circular pattern. The circles had precise edges and there was a sharp division between where the stalks had been laid and where they had not. It was as if some piece of precision machinery had swept the circles, yet it must have dropped out of the sky since the rest of the field was without blemish.

Since then Delgado has co-operated with others, notably Colin Andrews and a private pilot, F. C. ('Busty') Taylor, in sleuthing the increasing number and complexity of the shapes and patterns drawn in the fields of Wiltshire and Hampshire, while other groups have set themselves up elsewhere to investigate the examples in their own areas. The Delgado/Andrews/Taylor team, with help from others, has recorded from the air and on the ground a wealth of detail on what seems to be a phenomenon coming from an intelligent source (Delgado and Andrews, 1990).

Having probably as much knowledge and detachment as anyone, those mentioned above have come to the considered conclusion that whatever or whoever is responsible for the patterns is playing them along. For each year up to and including 1991 the patterns became more complex, culminating in the one that more than any other convinces me of their extraterrestrial origins. This was the Mandelbrot formation that appeared near Cambridge (Bartholomew, 1991).

If we needed any further proof that we were dealing here with the work of an advanced intelligence that has done all the same mathematical and scientific work as us and more, then the construction of this beautiful pattern gave it (Fig. 14.1). It was discovered by Beth Davis at Ickleton in Cambridgeshire on 12 August 1991 and was absolutely perfectly drawn looking from the air, like an artistic construction of carefully laid gold wire (Photo 8). The chances of this being a hoax are absolutely nil and it is, in my opinion, a waste of time to dwell on the matter. Whatever drew this, the most imaginably complex pattern in mathematics, knew exactly what it was doing and must have known that we had already produced it too (Bartholomew, 1991).

The design came as one aspect of the work of Benoit B. Mandelbrot, a research fellow at the IBM Thomas J. Watson Research Center in Yorktown Heights, New York. Mandelbrot has developed a mathematics called fractal geometry, which permits the study of forms having a fractional dimension (as opposed to, say, two or three dimensions, as areas and solids have). This complex field of study has become possible only since

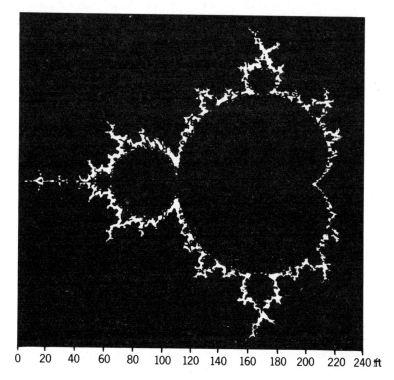

0 20 40 60 80 100 120 140 160 180 200 220 240 ft

Fig. 14.1 When plotted using a computer, the Mandelbrot Set produces this design. Comparison with Photo 7 shows that the crop design had every major feature of the computer plot, even down to having a dot off the end of the main scheme. The scale gives the size of the Ickleton crop plan.

the advent of computers and no one, however dedicated, could have hoaxed the design.

Mandelbrot's fractal geometry is used to study natural growth patterns and has a prominent place in so-called chaos theory. George Wingfield (Bartholomew, 1991) asks why the circle-makers should deal us a Mandelbrot Set pattern. As far as I am concerned, one answer is that I am (like many others) totally convinced of the extraterrestrial origin of these patterns. It also reinforces the contention, suggested by William Loosley's experience in the last century, that they have done it all before and so are not as alien as we might imagine. It also indicates that they are easily the equals of our most advanced mathematicians and scientists. I cannot resist the thought that they may be feeding us scientific ideas piece by piece – the way pure mathematicians have worked out the mathematical tools that will be necessary for the next generations of applied scientists is quite remarkable. In most cases, no application for their work is in sight when they do it. They are working for the pure love of discovering what can be done with numbers and symbols. Reading the history of scientific discovery, it is evident that the most important basic concepts in physics have come from 'inspirations' and not from the logical development of previous work. Newton's famous apple is just one example, but our inability since then to unlock the secrets of gravity indicates to me that we are not allowed to have it all. Anti-gravity machines could be bad not only for us but also for the 'Space Federation', so we do not get that vital bit of information. Having studied and taught physics for a long time, I feel sure that something of this kind is happening.

When we have pulled back one curtain, say Newton's, and worked out the consequences of what is revealed behind it, then another curtain, say Einstein's, is drawn aside. What is exciting at the moment in physics is the fact that we have gone about as far as the Einstein era will allow and we are due for the twenty-first century's curtain to be raised by someone who is probably alive today and maybe, unbeknown to them, already chosen and just waiting in the wings to be given the inspiration.

How They Might Do It

The gentle way the stalks of the crops are laid over at the point where they emerge from the ground is, for those versed in crop technology, one of the most remarkable of a very remarkable set of circumstances. What force could be used to do this?

Of the forces we know, electromagnetic force seems to be the best bet. The stalks could be laid if an electric current were induced in them. This would entail a fairly high voltage being developed between the top and bottom of the stalks, and there have been reports of cracklings associated with 'aura-like' lights in the vicinity of crop circles. Such cracklings could be the result of the high voltage.

Then a transverse magnetic field would be able to force the stalks over just as if they were wires in a strange kind of electric motor. Both the electric and magnetic effects could be fed down the same beam, which, apart from some light due to ionized air, would be invisible. Using its ability to remain invisible to the observer, the controlling UFO could be there as well. Only the wraith-like light and the cracklings would tell anyone that something odd was going on in the depths of the crop (Fig. 14.2).

Dowsing the Designs

A means by which genuine crop designs can be told from hoaxes is by dowsing. Apparently pendulums are the most effective means of evaluating the genuineness of a design. Those who think about the theory of the force that affects the dowsing rods, twig or pendulum are always, sometimes unscientifically, referring to magnetism. What they mean is not magnetism as obtained from magnets and electric currents, but a force which acts like magnetism does. This must be the case, as the materials used for dowsing are not magnetic themselves and therefore cannot respond to outside magnetism. Yet is the dowsing force something which is a consequence of electromagnetic lines of force? The fact is, we do not know, but Pat Delgado (Delgado and Andrews, 1990) tells us of his experiences with a pendulum in the circles and there is definitely something affecting the dowsing pendulum, even though he himself had never previously had any great success with dowsing by wire rods or twigs. We cannot imagine any residual magnetism being left in the ground of crop designs, because there is nothing there which could be magnetized. Yet something is there that affects the dowser and it would seem to follow the direction in which the crops are laid.

East Anglian Pictograms

Now that the designs drawn in the fields have become vastly more complex than mere circles, the term 'crop circles' seems rather out of date. A more accurate name for those very complex designs which form a kind of picture is 'pictograms'. Some we call agriglyphs, because we can make comparisons with glyphs from ancient languages (Bartholomew, 1991) and find that many designs bear a striking resemblance to some of them. However, as the most complex of the designs are so detailed and go well beyond the relative simplicity of single glyphs, the name pictogram has come into use; and within this general category, we get descriptive names like 'insectogram' and even 'violinogram'.

It is important to realize that designs have appeared in such diverse countries as Japan, Canada, Australia, the USA, Russia, Holland and Germany. Just as with the UFO phenomenon, the circles are found world-wide. However, it is only when you can inspect and measure the designs that appear on your doorstep yourself that you realize what a remarkable phenomenon they are.

The first design I was able to investigate personally was drawn in 1990 near Fordham Place, north of Colchester in Essex. It was

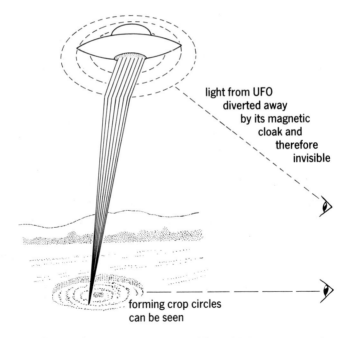

light from UFO
diverted away
by its magnetic
cloak and
therefore
invisible

forming crop circles
can be seen

Fig. 14.2 How an otherwise invisible UFO could draw the crop designs. The designs could be painted by an electromagnetic 'brush' controlled by some form of computer in the UFO. Using its gigamagnetic aura, the controlling craft could be invisible to anyone watching. The time to execute a design could be very short – maybe only a few seconds.

a perfect dumb-bell, with the bar connecting the two circles absolutely straight and clear-cut, and it was exactly 6 ft wide throughout its length (Photo 9). The precision of the laying was such that you could measure the dimensions to within an inch, and while the north and south circles were somewhat damaged by the combine harvester, it was easy to find that their diameters were, within reason, the same. Also there was no problem finding their centres, for this was occupied by a hole which, on probing with a rod, proved in both to be full of loose earth to a depth of 9½ in (Photo 10).

From the way the stalks were laid, it was evident that the south circle had been swept first, then the central bar made and the design completed by sweeping the north circle. However, there was a feature which made it quite evident that no one could possibly have hoaxed this design. Some way out from the centres the stalks were laid straight, but as one came in towards the holes the stalks had been bent in two or three places in order to conform to the small radius they were asked to follow (Photo 11). This is something which no hoaxer would have contemplated doing, if for no other reason than the prodigious amount of careful work it would have entailed.

What was remarkable about this design was the way it was repeated in the same place with a slightly different orientation in 1991, and to the same dimensions.

That same summer, on about 17 July 1991, a double feature appeared in a field at Reedlands Farm near Clacton, Essex. It consisted of a circle with a satellite dot and a triangle. Triangles will exhibit properties which circles cannot. They may have special proportions and special areas. They are also very difficult to hoax as the corners have to be cleanly cut, as they were at Reedlands. However, the circle was not simple, nor was its mode of formation.

A triangle, plus a circle of diameter 44 ft, was first noticed and at lunchtime that day Ronald West, a local crop-design investigator who runs the Essex UFO Research Group, went to look at it, taking some of his group with him. They had too short a time to investigate the circle and the triangle, so they decided to come back at tea-time. By the time they returned, a ring 1 ft wide had been drawn round the circle 5 ft from it (Photo 12). No one apparently saw anything strange going on during that July afternoon, but a crop-design maker had been there and had swiftly and unobtrusively swept this ring.

The triangle was also of great interest because its base was, at 17 ft 6 in, half of its height. One is reminded of the Cheesefoot circles of 1982, where the small ones were half the size of the large one. This triangle is special in that its area is the same as the square on its base.

However, an even more intriguing triangle turned up about 30 July 1991 as part of a complex design at the small hamlet of Akenham, 3 miles north of Ipswich, Suffolk. As shown in Fig. 14.3, there was a line of five circles with what might be the representation of an arrow through the centre one. Both the triangles which made the head and fleche of this arrow were special. The fleche triangle was probably meant to have angles of 45 to 90 degrees, but the head was vastly more intriguing. Both triangles had bases of 22 ft (which is the radius of the Reedlands Farm circle), but the height of the head triangle was 27 ft.

Now, it is well known that if you draw a triangle of the same proportions as a meridian cross-section of the Great Pyramid at Gizeh near Cairo – a pyramidal triangle as shown in Fig. 12.5 (a), – then twice the base (b) divided by the height (h) gives the value of *pi*. This is called the '*pi* proportion' and leads to the assertion that whoever designed the Great Pyramid effectively 'squared the circle', because if the perimeter (4b) of the base is considered equivalent to the circumference (c) of a circle and the height to its radius (r), then c/r gives the value 2*pi*. Also 4b/h gives 2*pi*. From this we get the so-called *pi*-proportion – i.e. $2b/h = pi$. Incidentally, as everyone learns at school, a good approximation for *pi* is 22/7 and it is remarkable how often 22 ft occurs in the dimensions of the crop designs. We see it several times in the circles and triangles of the designs mentioned above.

The remarkable thing about the Akenham triangle is that if you divide twice the base by the height (as we did to find the *pi*-proportion), then the result is the golden number (*phi*): 1.62 – the same number that is obtained from the Fibonacci series of numbers (see page 127).

Thus the head triangle at Akenham is very special indeed, but I believe it continues the UFO denizens' attempts to tell us that their mathematics and ours are the same. William Loosley might have recognized *phi* from the numbers he was given 120 years ago

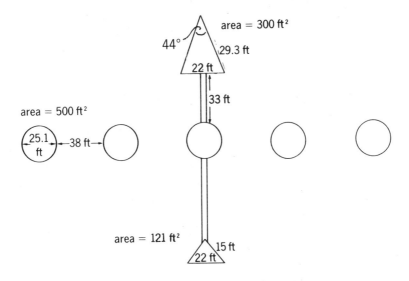

Fig. 14.3 The crop design at Akenham, Suffolk. Each of the circles had an area of 500 sq ft. The 'arrow' design had a 'fleche' triangle whose area was the same as a square on its height, but the arrowhead triangle was particularly special. Not only did it have an area of 300 sq ft but it had proportions that, when compared to the way the proportions of the Great Pyramid give *pi*, gave the golden number *phi*.

had he been a mathematician or if he had managed to contact an open-minded member of that breed. It is still being recorded for us today, but in a different way – a way that everyone can see, rather than just being given secretly to one person in one place.

Those who grab a calculator and punch in 44 divided by 27 will say that the value given for *phi* is closer to 1.63 than 1.62, but you have only to make the height between 2 and 3 in longer to get the exact figure and I submit that when drawn in standing corn, it is impossible to be sure of where an acute apex point ends to within 3 in or so. What is remarkable is that the precision is such that people feel they can measure the dimensions to quite close approximations. It is also useful to realize that the '*phi* triangle' has an angle of 44 degrees at the apex, continuing the play on 22.

Why UFOs?

The reader may well think that I have jumped the gun when I unequivocally attribute the crop designs to UFOs. The answer is that no theory fits the facts other than that the designs are being drawn by some form of electromagnetic beam controlled from an invisible UFO. It would appear from the available evidence that there may be an intermediate small kind of telemetry disc which occasionally can be seen actually doing the drawing, but it must, one imagines, receive its power down a beam projected from much higher up. However, the UFO is not always invisible. On at least one occasion a UFO has been caught in the act of making a circle.

It was the first report of a circle in England in 1991 and came from Butleigh in Somerset. A local lad, Dave Harris, was riding his bicycle towards Butleigh when he heard a high-pitched humming near an avenue of cedar trees which crossed the road. Some 25 ft up over a field of very early wheat to his left he saw a silvery bell-shaped craft. It was stationary and below it a spiralling vortex of 'aura-like' light was making a circle in the crop. Harris was so astounded by what he saw that he rode his bike into the side of the road and fell off on to the grass verge. The craft subsequently flew away at high speed and, apart from the hum, there was, Harris said, just a swishing noise as it departed. The whole thing was over in a few seconds. All this had taken place in broad daylight around 6 p.m. on Sunday, 14 April 1991 (Good, 1992).

Harris's description of the light as 'aura-like' indicates that it was not brightly luminous or clear-cut. Ionized air formed about a beam of strong EM radiation could produce a diffuse light like an aura. There was also the hum, which we can attribute to the skin waves in the magnetic shell surrounding the UFO playing on the surrounding air and so coming to Harris as a hum.

Other observations of UFOs in association with circles have occurred. Delgado and Andrews (1990) report that two pensioners, Pat and Jack Collins, were driving over Stockbridge Down in Hampshire on the evening of 6 July 1985 when they were extremely frightened by the appearance of a huge circular object standing on edge like a ferris wheel. It was stationary and hovering close to the ground some 200 yd from them. Yellow-white lights surrounded the rim of the object, while other lights formed spokes to the centre.

Groups of five crop circles were discovered the following morning near Alresford (12 miles east of Stockbridge) and at Goodworth Clatford (4½ miles north of Stockbridge). A similar form of sighting was made near Warminster in August 1982 and again there were crop circles in the vicinity.

This form of sighting is very unusual and it is doubtful if these wheel-like devices were busy making the circles that were afterwards found in the vicinity. However, they might conceivably be 'mother craft' providing back-up for the smaller UFO doing the actual work.

Strange Happenings

On Thursday, 22 October 1987, a Harrier jump-jet on a test flight from Boscombe Down ditched itself pilotless into the Atlantic some 500 miles from land. The flight was routine and the pilot, Taylor Humphrey Scott, was highly experienced. He had made a routine call to Boscombe control tower just before radio contact was lost at 5.06 p.m. It was at that moment the Harrier arrived over a crop-circle formation that had been made two months earlier in a field at Winterbourne Stoke. The body of the pilot was found the following evening in a field overlooking this crop formation with his secondary parachute nearby. His inflatable dinghy was in the corner of the field in which the formation had been made. As the ejector seat has never been found, it is conjectured that it remains in the ditched aircraft.

I do not know whether there were any mysterious circumstances surrounding the conditions in which the body was found, but how a pilot could bale out of a modern jet without his ejector seat and what caused him to do so anyway are unknown. Where was his main parachute and why did the aircraft change course by several degrees when it arrived over the field? Nobody knows the answers to these questions, but we cannot help remembering the other cases where aircraft have been sent off course because of interference with their compasses (Berlitz, 1975).

There have been other strange happenings experienced by the chief investigators of the crop designs. Delgado and Andrews (1990) tell of their compass spinning on one occasion and only one occasion. They have experienced sounds from invisible sources, even managing to record some of them on a tape-recorder, but the sounds and the events are ephemeral and once one kind has occurred it does not seem to re-occur. In other words, these odd events are not by-products of the means of formation of the circles. They are random in the way that things done by intelligent beings are random. You drop a book and make a noise. You do not repeat that error, because dropping books is not a good thing to do, but sometimes it happens. You may use an electric drill on one side of the house where you wish to install a screw for some purpose. If no other screw is required, that may be the only time for days that the noise of a drill will be heard in that locality. That is how intelligent beings operate. The noises they make or the effects they produce have meaning and purpose for them, but often there is no repeated pattern in what they do.

Thus it is with investigating the phenomena associated with UFOs. They are produced by intelligent beings for purposes which make sense to them but may make no sense at all to us. It is often quite useless to ask after a UFO event, 'Why did they do that?' because no useful answer will be forthcoming. Only when we have learned to communicate meaningfully with them will we be able to raise the veil of secrecy that pervades their operations on earth. Until that time, we can only observe, record and marvel at what they can do. Our scientific and technological revolution is helping us accept and even understand some of the manifestations that occur, yet when it comes to psychological events we are overwhelmed and alarmed by their methods and abilities. We have to accept that research in recent years has established that human beings are constantly being abducted, sometimes tagged and/or mentally programmed for reasons which it is often quite impossible to fathom. The dolphin fitted by us with an electronic transmitter has just as much idea of why this is being done as we have with UFOs – no more and no less.

CHAPTER
15

Mysteries Ancient and Modern

THE MOST ANCIENT detailed account of flying-saucer sightings we have comes from the Royal Annals of the pharaoh Thutmosis III (*c.* 1504–1450 BC). It comes from a translation of a damaged papyrus made by Prince Boris de Rachewiltz (Vallée, 1966).

In the year 22, of the third month of winter, sixth hour of the day . . . the scribes of the House of Life found it was a circle of fire that was coming in the sky . . . it had no head, the breath of its mouth had a foul odour. Its body one rod long and one rod wide. It had no voice. Their hearts became confused through it: then they laid themselves on their bellies . . . they went to the Pharaoh . . . to report it. His Majesty ordered . . . has been examined . . . as to all which is written in the papyrus rolls of the House of Life. His Majesty was meditating upon what happened. Now after some days had passed, these things became more numerous in the sky than ever. They shone more in the sky than the brightness of the sun, and extended to the limits of the four supports of the heavens . . . Powerful was the position of the fire circles. The army of the Pharaoh looked on with him in their midst. It was after supper. Thereupon, these fire circles ascended higher in the sky towards the south . . .

Here, some 3,500 years ago, are all the ingredients of a modern sighting of lights in the sky, both single and in formation.

They were circular and very bright. They made no noise and possibly the 'foul odour' was the smell of ionized air, which certainly has an unpleasant odour.

However, the most interesting thing is that the shape of saucers has not changed in all that time and their method of propulsion would also seem to be much the same, even though foul smells are not the normal accompaniment to close encounters these days. Certainly they had moved beyond the rocket stage of space travel, because the scribe was careful to record that no noise was heard.

There were reports through the following centuries of what we now, in view of our modern research into the phenomenon, recognize. In Japan on 23 August 1015, two objects were seen giving birth to smaller luminous spheres. A big cigar-shaped object was seen over France on 12 October 1527. In 1752 spheres coming out of a bright cylinder were reported over Angermanland, Sweden. On 30 August 1783, a very strange object emitted eight satellites over Greenwich Observatory in London and on 23 March 1877 at Vence in France fiery spheres which were extremely luminous came out of a cloud of peculiar shape and went slowly towards the north for an hour's duration (this last was reported in *L'Année Scientifique*, 1877, Vol. 5).

All these are Leviathan-like reports and they show there is no recognizable limit we can place on their first appearance over this planet. In fact, the Old Testament contains many examples of what would now be seen as UFO sightings and close encounters (Buttlar, 1979). There is a convincing body of evidence that the God of the Old Testament may have been represented by 'gods' from aerial craft who spoke with and directed the prophets, etc. in ways which must have been part of a plan. In other words, it was a time when the UFO denizens directly intervened in the affairs of human beings (Drake, 1968). For example, in Zechariah 5: 1–2 we find, 'Then I turned, and lifted up mine eyes, and looked, and behold a flying roll. And he said unto me, What seest thou? And I answered, I see a flying roll; the length thereof is twenty cubits, and the breadth thereof ten cubits.' An even better example comes from The Book of Ezekiel, in which aerial craft land and their occupants command Ezekiel to take certain communications to the leaders of his people. These visitations spanned a period of twenty-five years and Ezekiel's description of the details of the spacecraft he saw has enabled Josef Blumrich, a space engineer, to reconstruct the likely form of the craft (Blumrich, 1974).

UFO Navigation

As the alien spacecraft have been visiting us for so long, how have they navigated our skies? How indeed, in a largely virgin world, have they pinpointed where they are? Where are their beacons and flight corridors? Jacques Vallée (1967) takes a good critical look at the theory of orthoteny. This was first suggested by Aimé Michel and has been taken up by others. It seeks to prove that UFO sightings appear on straight lines when taken within the bounds of a country such as France or Spain, but may be in great circles when taken as a global phenomenon. This is what one might expect if UFOs fly definite corridors. Where such lines cross we might expect to find Ufocals (places which have a higher proportion of sightings than elsewhere). But when UFOs get to Ufocals, how do they know they are there and also how do they let themselves down from very high up in the right place?

Part of the answer may lie in something that has been revealed to me in an entirely different context over a period of many years. The first revelation came when I was making for Cradle Hill, to the north of Warminster. Cradle Hill is possibly one of the most prolific places for UFO sightings in the British Isles. People who have never seen UFOs anywhere else see them in this area. For example, Andrew Collins (1992) states that he saw the one and only UFO of his life while in the region of Upton Scudamore, a village a mile or so north-west of Cradle Hill (Fig. 15.1).

On the foggy evening of 9 October 1976 Collins and friends were on the A340 Warminster–Westbury road. By whim they took the farm track that leads away from Scudamore and into open land between Cradle Hill and Westbury. They were thus very close to Cradle Hill when they became aware of an intense ball of white light looming out of the fog from their right (the direction of Cradle Hill). They were on this occasion constrained largely to ignore the light and, after a somewhat frightening experience, they camped down for the night.

However, Arthur Shuttlewood (1976) describes a very similar light that he encountered in the same vicinity. Shuttlewood and

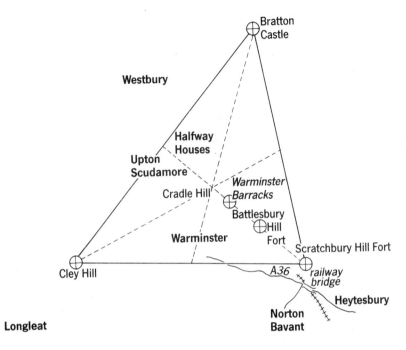

Fig. 15.1 The 'pyramid triangle' between Cley Hill, Bratton Castle and Scratchbury Hill Fort, showing how Cradle Hill lies at its centroid, how the aptly named Halfway Houses lie at the centre of the base and how Warminster Barracks lies on the line from Scratchbury to Cradle Hill. Places and positions where Annabelle Randall had her frightening encounters with aliens are shown in the lower right-hand corner, while Longleat estate is where other strange events occurred (see page 111).

his two colleagues said it was like a motorcycle headlamp or a circular lantern, and they were able to chase this manifestation as it changed shape from spherical to ovoid and at one time 'danced up and down like a yo-yo'. The object was obviously intelligently controlled, for it led them a merry dance through copses and fields before it outdistanced them and they lost it.

These are just two instances of strange manifestations near Cradle Hill, and it was a reference to UFOs seen there that had me poring over a map. I found Cradle Hill, but something else of greater wonder caught my eye. I suddenly realized that this

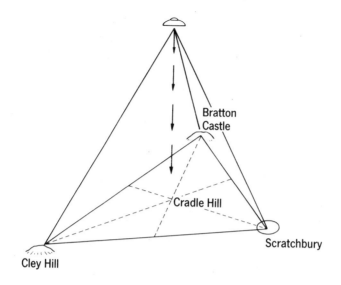

Fig. 15.2 A possible way in which such an exact triangle could be used as an automatic 'window' for UFOs letting down from space. The UFOs would naturally appear over Cradle Hill.

Ufocal lay near the centre of a triangle formed by Cley Hill, Bratton Castle and Scratchbury Hill Fort (Fig. 15.2). The triangle was, I thought, something I recognized from reading *The View Over Atlantis* (Michell, 1969). It was indeed a very special shape, which I will call a 'pyramidal triangle' because it had the same proportions as a meridian cross-section of the Great Pyramid of Cheops at Gizeh, near Cairo.

Even more astonishing was how accurate the triangle proved to be. The highest point of Cley Hill to the long barrow within the ramparts of Bratton Castle formed a baseline which was exactly 5 nautical miles (Nmi) long, while both the slant sides (apothems) were 4 Nmi. The height-line of this precise triangle passed straight through Cradle Hill, and the Field Barn on it lies at the centroid of the triangle (the point where the lines from the corners to the centres of the opposite sides meet).

At the bottom of the height-line lies Halfway Houses, close to Upton Scudamore. Could they be so called because they lie exactly half-way along this triangle's baseline? It was close to here that both Collins and Shuttlewood had their UFO sightings.

Many other strange events have occurred close to points of this triangle. Warminster Barracks, where the garrison was shaken from their beds on Christmas morning 1964 (Chapter 2), lies directly under the height-line and half-way between Battlesbury and Cradle Hill. Close to the south of the apex (Scratchbury Hill) lies the little village of Norton Bavant.

Miss Annabelle Randall had some strange experiences between the latter two places on the night of Thursday, 7 October 1965. Driving her fiancé, John, home from Warminster towards Heytesbury on the A36, she was negotiating a particularly difficult railway bridge under the shadow of Scratchbury when she was forced to swerve to avoid what both she and John thought was an inert man sprawled well out into the road. Thinking it was a drunken soldier, John ran back to investigate and found to his amazement and alarm that there was no sign of the man – no bloodstains from an injury, nothing! Only a few seconds elapsed between leaving the car and reaching the spot. He then searched the area for over ten minutes before giving up, now almost convinced that they had seen a ghost.

But Annabelle's ordeals were not over. Having dropped John, she was driving back and nearing the same bridge, but from the east this time, when she became aware of a bright-orange glow close to the railway embankment. It was, she said (Shuttlewood, 1967):

> a large orange ball. I had changed down a gear to take the bridge, yet the engine at full throttle was missing and conking out. For a moment, as I drove over the bridge, I had the impression of being pushed backwards. My full-beam headlights dimmed, flickering like a candle in the wind. This caused me nearly to hit the bank, with the motor suddenly coughing and spluttering. I literally crept along the short stretch of road towards the left-hand turning to Norton Bavant. I kept my foot hard down all the way. I was almost blinded by the dazzling ball of light to my right.
>
> Just beyond the junction with the Bavant road, an unlit vehicle was parked. What sort it was I really do not know, apart from it having a circular shape. I could not clearly pick out any discernible features, because the light from the

opposite side was so powerful. It was glaring and hurt my eyes, yet cast a haze over the roadway. That may sound a paradox but it is true.

Then the thing spun into the road in front of me and my engine stopped altogether. There was no need for me to slam on my brakes, although I did so automatically. I saw red and blue sparks fly from the spinning rim of whatever it was. Then, bright crimson in colour, it flew off at a tangent to my right. From the corner of my eye I noticed it blaze a trail in the sky.

Then an already terrifying experience was made more horrific because two people appeared in front of her. As they were in the middle of the road, Annabelle nearly bowled them over, having to swerve to avoid them. Because they wore dark woollen balaclavas, she thought they were soldiers on a night exercise. She could see only their noses and the suspicion of eyes – widely spaced and deep sunk in the classic alien mould. They also had the skin-tight, dark clothes usually associated with aliens. She described their lower garments as being like a skin-diver's or frogman's. She concluded, probably rightly, that the two figures came from the immobile vehicle – if that is what it actually was.

At another time, Shuttlewood tells of a man being overtaken on the open road in the vicinity of Warminster by an unlit box-like vehicle which became enveloped in a yellow mist and then literally vanished before his eyes. Such tales, while bizarre, are not so impossible or rare as to throw doubts on the sanity of the incredulous observers.

However, now that the orange object had departed Annabelle's car ran, as we have come to expect, perfectly normally and she sped home as fast as she could, her heart pounding wildly.

We have seen much of this before. The extremely luminous 'mass' that exhibits bright colours and radiates the electromagnetic aura that interferes with the ignition of cars at some distance was discussed in Chapter 9. The 'haze' over the roadway which so perplexed Annabelle was probably the result of refraction in the strong magnetic beam being projected from the UFO which eventually stopped her car (see page 49). The events surrounding alien 'soldiers' are more perplexing, but not unlike many of the close-encounter experiences of others (Puharich, 1974 and Strieber,

1989, for example). It seems that those Whitley Strieber prefers to call 'visitors' have the most amazing abilities with the creation and subsequent annihilation of apparently real objects and even creatures, such as whatever it was that lay half off the pavement and looked so real that it forced Annabelle to swerve. Yet was that any more than a projection, a holographic show for these two frightened people for purposes we can only guess at? Was Annabelle 'targeted'? After all, she was the participant in the second encounter and it is becoming abundantly clear that UFO events do not happen at random. There is purpose behind them.

These bizarre cases serve to illustrate that the area bounded by what we will call the 'Warminster Triangle' is one where UFOs disport themselves. I began to think that the three points forming the exact corners of this triangle were perfect devices for some form of radar-like positioning set-up that would automatically let the UFOs down over its centroid: Cradle Hill. Was this indeed one reason for our ancient monuments being where they are? Did hilltops, barrows and high-points in later forts form special positions possibly laid down as navigation 'beacons' in the remote past and are they still in use today? Is the basic shape of Cheop's pyramid vastly older than the date attributed to it by Egyptologists? And even more heretical – was the shape in use in Britain before its use in Egypt? The implications are enormous, but just as one swallow does not make a summer, so one triangle does not make a theory. Maybe it was just pure coincidence.

It was the way Arthur Shuttlewood fled from the publicity that surrounded his contribution on 'The Thing' in the *Daily Mirror* in September 1965 that led us to think that maybe this was somewhat more than coincidence.

His parents were at Chelmsford and so he escaped there to let the furore die down, but he recalls what a remarkably strong feeling he had that he must visit West Mersea, south of Colchester. Now, this is my area as well. On getting married, my wife and I lived for two years in part of a sixteenth-century house on Mersea Island and within a stone's throw of the great mound called the Mersea Barrow. Shuttlewood (1967) describes how on 13 September 1965 he tried vainly to catch a bus to Mersea but for some strange reason a series of coincidences meant that he never made it. He wanted to see the area that is called Wick – an open area of agricultural land and salt flats to the north of the arm of the sea that makes Mersea an island. This was a rather odd desire, because the area is quite desolate, but it might have something to do with someone I know quite well, Paul Green, who at the time lived with his parents on Mersea Island.

It was early the next morning, at about 1.30 a.m., that Paul was riding his motorcycle home after seeing his fiancée, who lived in Colchester. The road from Colchester to Mersea is one I know very well having used it regularly. Thus when Paul told me his story I knew exactly where things had happened.

There is a straight portion of this road (Fig. 15.3) which goes past Pete Tye Common. It was here that he experienced a high-pitched humming which, as it grew louder, he connected to a small pinpoint of light coming in from the east over Brightlingsea. The light became rapidly larger as the noise changed to a high-pitched buzz. Then the engine of his bike began to cough and then stopped dead. His lights also went out.

He saw that the light was on the dome of an enormous saucer, whose diameter he estimated to be about 70 ft. It had what he described as a 'ball race' underneath around the rim and in the centre a large orifice that wreathed 'smoke' (Fig. 15.4). He had pulled his immobile bike on to its stand and, mesmerized and unable to speak, watched the pulsating blue light, the intensity of which was painful: 'It appeared to fluctuate in rhythm with my heartbeat and hit against my chest. I felt myself tingling all over – rather like an electric shock. The buzzing then became quieter and the object descended into the area of Wick.'

Having a superior machine, he had, just before the encounter, overtaken a boy on a scooter. This lad now came up but, running into the corridor of immobility, his engine and lights also failed. Neither of them said a word to the other as they stared petrified at the blue light. Then Paul's head began to throb and a tight band seemed to develop round it. With great effort he forced himself to move, kicked the bike back into life and roared off home, still aware of the blue light over the intervening hedges.

He experienced some recurrence of the sensations in a cinema the following evening and about a fortnight later the seams of his biking jacket weakened and fell apart. There would seem to be some 'missing time' in this experience, as the account in *Flying Saucer Review* (Finch, 1965) states that Paul had his experience at

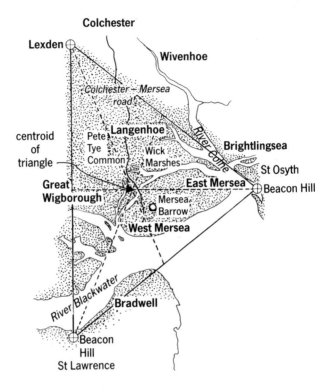

Fig. 15.3 Map of the area to the south of Colchester, Essex, showing Wick Marshes, where the Langenhoe saucer landed. Also the Beacon Hill 'triangle', whose centroid is close to Wick and Mersea Island, where the author saw his first UFO.

1 a.m., while he told me it was 1.30 a.m. and he says he did not arrive home until 2 a.m. Under normal circumstances it could not have taken a full hour for the UFO to approach and stop his bike, and for him to get going and ride rapidly home – a journey of, at the most, ten to fifteen minutes. This suggests that he had possibly been 'tagged' during the experience, for he has had at least one 'visitation' by a space denizen subsequently.

The region of Wick, out on the Langenhoe Marshes, is in many ways akin to Cradle Hill at Warminster. There is an ancient town nearby but the position is otherwise desolate – a perfect place for a Ufocal.

162

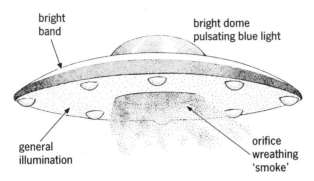

Fig. 15.4 Drawing of the Langenhoe saucer as described to the author by Paul Green. Its diameter was, according to Green, about 70 ft.

I know from gathering reports for many years that Mersea and the surrounding area are a prolific source of UFO sightings. The first UFO I ever saw was over the ancient East Mersea church. A lady at West Mersea reported in 1967 what had to be a Leviathan moving in and out of cloud without sound: she said it was silvery and of giant proportions. On Tuesday, 19 September 1967, Heather Pavitt, then a student at the local technical college, said that at about 10.30 p.m. she saw from her home at Wivenhoe a light suddenly appear as if 'set off like a firework'. Very bright, it started falling in an arc with a white trail behind it; the light had a red aura. It then slowed in its fall and the trail suddenly disappeared. It then changed to a very bright red light, after which the object turned and the red light began to go on and off. The whole observation lasted for some two minutes. The direction of the observation shows it to be somewhere over the same area as Paul Green's experience.

These are just a few of the sightings that have occurred in the area. They may not be as prolific as those associated with Cradle Hill, but there are sufficient to justify the contention that this desolate area of Essex is one where UFOs are seen more often than elsewhere in the vicinity.

Just as at Warminster, there is a pyramidal triangle covering this area of Essex and it exists between three important ancient points (see Fig. 15.3). Two of them are still called Beacon Hill. The one that forms the apex of the triangle is on the foreshore at

St Osyth; the other forming the lower corner is at St Lawrence, not far from the Bradwell nuclear power station. The last point is at Lexden, the original seat of kingship at Colchester, close to the parish church.

These three form a perfect triangle, with sides that are measured in numbers like those in the Warminster triangle, but the unit in which they are measured is different. The 'Mersea Triangle' has a centroid that lies close to the ancient causeway called the Strood, which just prevents Mersea being a total island. It is close enough to Wick Marshes and other points where UFOs have been seen for it to be put forward as a possible Ufocal.

Another researcher into great triangles laid out on the English countryside has connected Warminster and Mersea Island, via part of the baseline of one of Philip Heselton's 'Great Isosceles Triangles'. Heselton discovered these when looking for straight-line relationships between antiquities – i.e. leys. Having personally studied leys for a number of years, I am convinced that they exist, but as yet there is no convincing theory as to their use.

If such earth-mystery figures are connected with UFO navigation, then the undoubted feeling among researchers, that there is a connection between UFOs and ancient sites, is strengthened. It has been particularly noted how crop designs seem to appear close to sites of antiquity. Wiltshire has more ancient sites than any other county in England and it also spawns the most prolific crop designs, as well as some of the most complex.

Yet, having said this, the fact remains that many of the things connected to UFOs are so ephemeral and exhibit so many facets, it is extremely difficult to convince people one way or the other.

CHAPTER 16

The Mind-benders

Back in 1982 in the small Suffolk town of Hadleigh a strange thing happened. Mavis Burrows, a psychic and healer with no previous artistic ability, received 'instructions from elsewhere' to gather drawing boards, pens, coloured pencils and an odd assortment of tin lids, etc., and to compose some wonderful examples of 'space art'.

Each of the big 'canvases' was 2 ft wide by 1 ft 10 in high and eventually there were fourteen of them. Each took her, on average, about two solid hours of work. In addition there were some twenty smaller drawings done on cartridge paper.

Two technological examples of Mavis's 'space art' are shown in Photos 13 and 14. Here we find what look like buildings with superstructures and sprouting from their tops are apparently some form of broadcasting antennae. Up in the air are some strange moon-like devices, but in Fig. 16.1, among almost nothing that is recognizable, something appears that we have seen before. In the circular arrangement that might be some form of TV screen we see a representation of a Leviathan. It has the familiar light patches down the side and the 'submerging submarine' stance that is so often reported, and it hovers apparently over a landscape with a mound and a road to the mound. The rows of dots around the strange antenna coming from the back of the Leviathan might possibly be radiation, which is absorbed by the different atmosphere shown in red on the original. As well as this, there are some symbols. One may represent a serpent, but the other occurs time and again through the drawings. It is repeated, one notices, in the lower segment of the curious semicircular space at bottom right, but this is some form of semiogram (ideogram) as the basic shape is altered subtly with extra strokes and an array of dots.

That these drawings were 'automatic' (an artistic form of automatic writing) is proved by the fact that the angles between the various lines are often so meaningful. They are in several cases the base angle (just less than 52 degrees) of the Great Pyramid. Often we get exact 30- and 60-degree angles, as well as the 35 degrees associated with Imhotep and the Step Pyramid at Saqqara. Saqqara is the name of the village but takes its name from Saqar, the Egyptian 'god' of orientation. Imhotep was the fabulous architect of King Zoser and was himself worshipped as a demi-god because of his abilities. One of the Mavis Burrows designs investigated by the author fits into a grid of two sets of lines and the angle between the two sets is this same 35 degrees. It thus explains in some way why Mavis Burrows was given two clues as to the means of unravelling the conundrum that had been bequeathed to her. She was furnished with the name of Imhotep and also 'told' that the works had something to do with crop circles.

Fig. 16.1 In one of Mavis Burrows's drawings a large 'pyramid' appears covered in the symbols that pervade many of her other drawings (compare Fig. 16.3). They do not appear to be like those of Adamski and Homet (see Figs. 4.2 and 4.3) or Granchi (see Fig. 12.6).

That is how I became involved. I had written a letter to the Royal Meteorological Society's magazine *Weather*, pointing out that the crop-design phenomenon had outstripped a purely meteorological explanation. This was picked up by Dennis Hopper, the agricultural correspondent of the *East Anglian Daily Times*, who did an article about the phenomenon and my views on it. This in turn was read by Mavis Burrows, who felt she had to bequeath these drawings that had 'something to do with crop circles' to me. I am fully mindful of the privileged position in which I have been placed and have been working on the drawings since then with the few clues I have been given.

One way in which the Mavis Burrows space art could be connected to the crop designs lies in the glyphs that pervade them. In one drawing there is a marvellous pyramid covered in 'boxes', each of which contains a glyph (Fig. 16.1). Some of these glyphs are repeated and some are altered slightly by the addition of dots. Many of the more complex designs drawn in our fields have dots associated with them. In at least one case a dot has been added after the design was drawn as if to change its meaning (Bartholomew, 1991). However, while certain of the characters in the Burrows drawings have been seen elsewhere, taken as a whole they seem to represent a new language.

We can, nevertheless, find certain correspondences. For example, there is a certain resemblance between two of the simpler glyphs and a space design given in *Alien Contact* (Randles and Whetnell, 1991). On 24 June 1979 the teenage daughter of the Sunderland family had a form of 'transportation' experience in which she found herself passing through a tunnel into a beautiful country landscape. Around her, she said, there were curly-leaved flowers not unlike snapdragons with warm soft colours. Despite being only in her nightdress she felt 'wrapped in a cocoon of warmth'. She was confronted by an alien family (man, woman and child), the adults of which she had encountered in a previous visitation. The circular badge shown in Fig. 16.2 was carried by all of them on the left breast. The man said he was Parz and the woman Arna. They then proceeded to show Gaynor their city. We do not have enough space here to give any more information about this encounter, but it is of interest that the proportions of the triangular shapes given in *Alien Contact* are almost exactly the same as those of the pyramid in Fig. 16.1.

Fig. 16.2 The 'space badges' worn by the aliens encountered by a member of the Sunderland family. They include the question-mark and wave symbols seen in Figs. 16.3 and 16.5.

To illustrate some more of the many glyphs in Mavis Burrows's drawings another squat pyramid is shown in Fig. 16.3. We see the wave and the question-mark glyphs in all these three examples. Only one or possibly two of the Granchi symbols (see page 131) appear to be the same as the Burrows glyphs, but the former bear a much greater resemblance to the symbols of the Adamski/Homet language (see page 41).

Michael Green (Bartholomew, 1991) makes a convincing case for the resemblance of many of the crop designs (treated now as the symbols of a language and called agriglyphs) to the symbols found by a nineteenth-century French archaeologist on the Canary Island of Fer. At a place aptly named Los Leteros he discovered an area of basaltic lava with a smooth surface on which inscriptions had been engraved. The glyphs covered an area which was roughly 1,200 ft across. Green says that many of the Fer symbols are the same as the Granchi ones.

Despite all these various sources of ancient ideograms and glyphs, none of them really convincingly ties up together so that we can say that any two represent the same language. Even if we find the same shapes, this does not mean they represent the same language, for we only have to look at our own modern languages. Take French and German. German is unintelligible to the French if they have not studied the Germanic language, and vice versa,

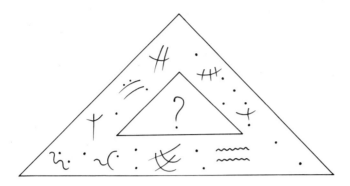

Fig. 16.3 Another 'pyramid' from Burrows's drawings. In these the dots would appear to convey shades of meaning in the glyphs, just as the dots accompanying agriglyphs may, once we understand them, alter their meaning.

yet both (with a few exceptions) are written in the same Roman characters. Then the cursive scripts of Arab countries are wholly foreign to Europeans, and if Arabs and Europeans sent space expeditions using their own languages anyone on another planet, unless told otherwise, might be forgiven for thinking that they came from entirely different source planets.

In Photo 14 the somewhat bird-like device within the circle below the lens-shaped 'craft' is not entirely unknown to us. We find extensive use of the same kind of imagery on Hopi Indian pottery taken from the mound of Sikyatki (Fig. 16.4) (Fewkes, 1973). The Hopi are the most ancient tribe of Pueblo Indians that can be traced and it is of considerable interest to find that tradition records their original ancestors as coming 'down in a whirlwind'. This allusion to whirlwinds is also found in similar circumstances in the Old Testament, where, according to the Second Book of Kings (2:11): 'And it came to pass, as they still went on, and talked, that, behold, there appeared a chariot of fire, and horses of fire, and parted them both asunder; and Elijah went up by a whirlwind into heaven.'

Earlier still, the Patriarch Enoch, said in Genesis to have been the father of Methuselah, was, at the end of his 365 years on earth, also said to have been transported to heaven in a whirlwind. Undoubtedly, any descents or ascents to hovering spacecraft would have been likened to the way quite heavy objects can be taken up and let down again in tornadoes and lesser whirlwinds. Even Christ went the same way – taken up into a cloud before the astonished eyes of the onlookers.

My view of the Mavis Burrows phenomenon is that we have here something which we may one day understand but which is far ahead of its time. Alternatively, at some time in the future someone will be 'visited' by aliens and transported to the drawings' planet of origin or to its space station so that they can explain what to us is at present quite incomprehensible. Well, not entirely incomprehensible. Odd clues peep through the fog of ignorance.

In the other technological Burrows drawing (see Photo 14) we have what looks like a building with its strange antennae, plus the obviously important bi-convex 'craft'. Possibly the 'feather' design in the sphere below depicts the passage of a spacecraft through space. We do, however, have a source of information about the big lens-shaped device.

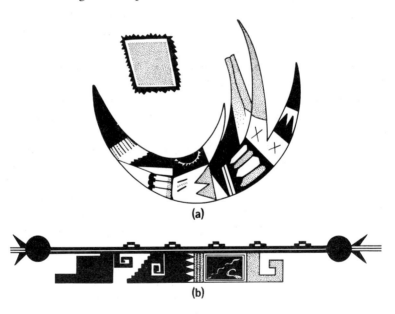

(a)

(b)

Fig. 16.4 (a) A so-called 'feather design' from pottery unearthed at the Hopi settlement of Sikyatki. Compare the similar design in Fig. 16.2. **(b)** Linear motives on Hopi pottery are very reminiscent of the 'buildings' in the Burrows drawings (after Fewkes, 1973).

Robert Charroux (1972) describes his interrogation of a certain Mn. Y, who, like Meier (Kinder, 1987), claims to have been transported to a planet, in this case Baavi in the Alpha group of Centaur A and B. To convince Charroux that he was indeed under the tutelage of beings from Baavi, Mn. Y produced extensive documentation – so vast a documentation, indeed, that Charroux is of the opinion that no one individual could possibly have invented, first, the story of the journey to Baavi; second, an almost complete grammar of the Baal language of Baavi; and third, descriptions of inter-galactic spacecraft and more. Thus, single-handedly, Mn. Y had, if he was a hoaxer, to have invented a full new language with syntax and grammar; a large amount of advanced science; a system of weights and measures and of time, plus much philosophy and ethics. Charroux concluded that it was more plausible to accept that Mn. Y had had the experiences that he claimed.

Among these was his story of the interplanetary journey in a 'vaid' or vaidorge – a form of spacecraft. He spent two months on Baavi and certainly he disappeared for that two months, as his family thought him dead and went into mourning for him. The interplanetary journey occupied one and a half hours. Mn. Y says that they flew 'at more than gravific speed and then we were in anti-time'. Fig. 16.5 is a drawing of a vaidorge based on Charroux's book and it will be seen that the device in Photo 14 has the same convex lens shape and a circular (actually spherical) area in the centre.

In his testimony Mn. Y calls this spherical central volume 'the navigation cabin'. He says:

> The navigation cabin is spherical, transparent from within but opaque from the outside; it is isothermal and resistant to both light rays and radiation; light can be seen from the interior but this interior is itself dark.
>
> Inside is a central sphere some 5 ft in diameter, which contains only the ship's instruments, the navigational aids and protosynthetic machinery. The central sphere is also the actual stabilizing mechanism; it prevents the ship from reacting to any giratory movement of the disc which may be caused by the cosmic forces of turbulence . . . Everything in this cabin is weightless, so seats, etc., would be of no use.

A vaid cannot stand on the ground, but it can be made to hover steadily at 4 or 5 ft above ground by making certain adjustments at the gate-lock.

In the earlier chapters of this book I have put forward a theory based on known physical principles which could account for many of the effects shown by UFOs. However, I am fully aware that these known effects could be secondary to something more advanced of which we are, as yet, unaware. Certainly there has to be a super-Einstein physics which will confer on us some knowledge of anti-gravity. On this aspect Mn. Y has the following to say:

Modification of gravific waves is affected by twenty-four lenses (twelve on either side of the disc) that switch on the apparatus. The various evolutions – starting, sudden stoppage, enormous acceleration – are controlled by a titanium ring 'swimming' in a tube. [Could this be the tube shown in Photo 14 at the bottom of the central sphere?]

Gravific power, when used, acts simultaneously on every part of the ship and on everything within its sphere of influence.

If a vaid is to be brought down from a height to less than about 14,000 ft, an artificial electric charge produced by the rotation of the disc is brought into action. The autonomous electricity is adjusted to the gravitational field of the planet that is to be visited.

A vaid can travel at more than the speed of light, at even more than the speed of gravific waves, although these move seventeen times faster than light.

Here we see that at present there is no way we can accept or deny what Mn. Y states. We do not yet know the connection between electromagnetism and gravity that is implied when it is said that the electric charge of the vaid is adjusted to the gravity of the planet. However, the statements are somewhat imprecise and so we might interpret this as saying that our theory of electromagnetic propulsion is maybe not too far off the mark. We needed enough electrons to hit the underside of the top surface of the magnite sandwich that formed the bell surface of the saucer in order to counteract gravity. Is that what Mn. Y's statement actually means?

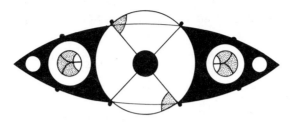

Fig. 16.5 A cross-section of a 'vaid' or 'vaidorge'. Compare the device in Fig. 16.2 and also the 'whirling arms' device in Fig. 4.2.

The statement goes on to discuss the state of the vaid at speeds greater than that of light. It is said to function in 'negative time', although the occupants' own biological clocks continue to act as normal.

Above the speed of light, the Einstein mass-energy relationship no longer applies. When the vaid attains the speed of light (or maybe from M's testimony (Puharich, 1974), 99 per cent of that speed), then a change comes over it and it makes a quantum jump into a new physical realm. It is like the electron in an atom, transferring from one orbit to another with a consequent change of potential energy.

Once in this new realm there will be no need to move into a higher realm unless the light distance to be covered demands it. The statement concludes by saying that we have to realize that vaids are not powered by engines in the usual sense of the word, nor 'by any mechanism intended to counteract the pull of forces within one's normal experience'.

The vaid is an inter-stellar spacecraft and will almost certainly be more sophisticated in its propulsion system than most of the 'scout' craft that emanate from Leviathans. However, the device in both Adamski's and Homet's drawings (see Figs. 4.2 and 4.3) shows a basic shape very similar to the conventional drawing of a vaid.

Thus maybe some saucers that show the effects we described in earlier chapters, and for which we tried to give rational explanations within the realms of modern physical knowledge, could be powered by an electromagnetic drive. Meanwhile, the devices designed to cover the light distances between planets of the galaxy are using a form of gravity drive. The fact is that we do not know much about any of these things, but the evidence we have, sparse as it is, does make some sense to us today, whereas when the phenomenon really hit the headlines, just post-war, it could not have done so in the same way.

There is definite evidence from those who have driven cars close to UFOs that not only was the electrical system of the car affected but a gravity-like physical force prevented them from approaching too close to the UFO. For example, during the frightening experience of Annabelle Randall, described in Chapter 15, her car not only spluttered and died but she had no need to brake, for the car slowed of its own accord, as if the brakes had been applied.

Clues such as the Leviathan and vaid representations in Mavis Burrows's art indicate to me that the originator was someone from the realms of the UFOnauts. While she herself is highly psychic, this does not mean that these drawings came from a spirit entity. Mavis's heightened awareness could well have just made her a good contact and someone capable of translating these highly complex drawings on to paper, even though she herself had shown no previous artistic ability.

Pictograms that have appeared in our fields in 1991 and 1992 offer connections between UFOs, pictograms and Mavis Burrows's drawings. At Lockeridge, near Marlborough, Wiltshire, what has been described as a 'whalogram' was drawn in a wheat field on the night of 30 July 1991 (Fig. 16.6). Just two days later, on 1 August, a similar design appeared at Firs Farm, Beckhampton, close to Avebury (Bartholomew, 1991).

These designs may, I feel, be symbolic of vaids, for, as the diagram shows, there is a circle drawn in the centre of the lens-shaped body of the design. Possibly the two rings represent the planets of origin and arrival. They were identical in design, but what the 'wings' indicate is not certain. Two other 'whale' designs appeared nearby, one at Hungerford and another at Firs Farm again. In these cases, the ends of the body either broke into or contacted the circles, the wings were missing and dots were drawn where the extensions of the bodies contacted the outer edges of the circles.

When Mavis Burrows said to me that her drawings had something to do with crop circles, I began to look for things she

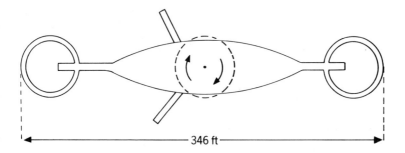

Fig. 16.6 A crop design formed at Lockeridge near Marlborough, Wiltshire, in 1991 may be a representation of a vaid travelling from planet A to planet B.

had habitually drawn turning up in the crop designs. The most prolific symbol that pervades the drawings is a thin crescent and until 1992 this device had not appeared in any of the crop-design publications. Then the design sketched in Fig. 16.7 appeared in Martineau (1992). This was drawn in wheat at West Stowell, Wiltshire, on 3 August. The crescent is very like those in Figs. 16.1 and 16.2, and maybe as time goes on other symbols that appear in Mavis's drawings will turn up in the fields of Britain and the world.

The apparently psychic elements in some UFO close encounters do not mean that UFOs are some strange warps of the human mind. *Homo sapiens* has made great strides with the studies of inanimate matter, but has only begun to brush the surface of the study of the mind.

If anything truly differentiates the UFO denizens from us it is their mastery of the mind. We now have a significant and growing number of testimonies to the ways they have of achieving their objectives by 'taking over' certain individuals.

For example, in his remarkable book *Intruders*, Budd Hopkins (1988) describes the way that Kathie Davis was tagged and followed through her life, culminating in her being used as a surrogate mother for an alien-human cross – a girl called Emily (Hopkins changed the names). To those who have not read Hopkins's book, or any of the other similar events that have overtaken certain 'abductees', this will seem absolutely crazy, but there is now too

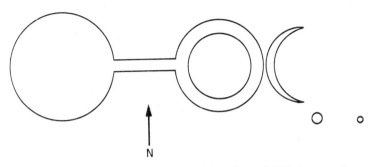

Fig. 16.7 The crop design drawn at West Stowell, Wiltshire, on 3
August 1992 is the first to show a thin crescent – a motif that pervades
Mavis Burrows's drawings. Once again, satellite dots are present.

much evidence for the phenomenon to be dismissed out of hand. It
will be dismissed out of hand by many people unable to cope with
the implications, but that will not stop it being the truth. Some
human beings, maybe many throughout the world, are marked for
purposes we can often only begin to guess at. In the case of Kathie
Davis, there is some explanation – a mentally advanced but poor
physical race could be trying to improve its stock. In other cases
there seems to be little understanding of the motives for abducting
and often clinically investigating certain human beings. In the case
of the young man Antonio Villas Boas, described by Hopkins (see
also Buttlar, 1979), there seems to be real evidence that he was
'forced' to have sexual intercourse with an alien female. This might
be another way of improving a poor physical race, because despite
our mental backwardness humanity is very beautiful physically and
it would seem that certain of the space races envy this and would
wish to emulate it.

The reader can become convinced of the truth of the
abduction and infiltration cases only by reading the evidence for
themselves. Then they may be in a position to say that it is all
bunkum. However, like me, who came to the abduction cases
with a very open mind, they may well become converted to
believing that these things are going on. That they are also
associated with UFOs is beyond doubt. For instance, the
frontispiece of *Intruders* contains this quote: 'Me and Mom are
hiding in the closet because there's a big thing in the sky, and

Mom is real scared. Then suddenly she's pulled from the closet and I'm terrified that I'll never see her again.' Mom *is* seen again, but that does not stop those caught up in such nightmares being scared out of their wits. As such the forces among us are alien. Only after a long process of 'education' and acceptance did people like Whitley Strieber (1987, 1989) come to call their unknown companions 'visitors'; the rest will see them as unfeeling aliens.

This last fact makes me realize that true contact, with the space races visiting us, is a very long way off, if it ever comes about. However, during the long, slow apprenticeship that will precede our graduating to the guilds of the 'Space Federation', we can expect many more odd and curious encounters with many things we do not understand. It will be a painful process and both scientists and political-cum-military powers will have to abandon entrenched power struggles and become humble before the 'Lords of the Heavens' before it can truly happen.

CHAPTER 17

What are They Telling Us?

I LOOKED AT my dog Boffin the other day and suddenly realized a great truth. Boffin does not want to go to the moon.

In fact, I would consider that Boffin does not want to do anything but be a dog on this solid old earth; and all other animals are probably the same. Only humans have the wish or the potential to get off this planet and seek other worlds. I saw just what this could mean. Deep within us we must have the desire to return whence we came.

If, as seems probable, animals are natural products of earth evolution, then if *Homo sapiens* had not happened along all the orbs of the universe might as well not be there. All earth's creatures would be forever incarcerated on this planet, with neither the wish nor the ability to go anywhere else. Yet humans have this quest for the stars.

Only humans, as far as we can tell, think about life on other worlds. Only humans look into the night and wonder who inhabits the planets of the stars that twinkle in the firmament. Only our as yet restricted technology prevents us reaching out to seek adventure, first on the nearer planets of our own solar system and then on the planets of nearby solar systems.

This kind of reasoning, to me, lends credence to the contention that it is human-like beings that are visiting us. The available evidence seems to suggest that human-like entities people the planets of those nearer stars which are in the correct physical positions compared to their own 'suns' to sustain life.

When Alice Wells, one of the witnesses of the encounter

between a spaceman and George Adamski, made a sketch of the contacting entity, it was November 1952. Very similar-looking men were reported by Mrs Jenny Roestenburg, looking at her out of transparent panels in a disc-shaped object that hovered over her house on 21 October 1954. This happened at Ranton near Shrewsbury at 4.45 p.m. and she described the men as having white skins, long hair to their shoulders and foreheads so high that all their features appeared to be in the lower half of their faces. They wore transparent helmets and turquoise-blue clothing like ski suits (Bowen, 1969). Apart from the very high foreheads, these details were shared by Adamski's contactee quite closely.

One of the most consistently reported forms of human-like creature seen in association with landed UFOs is what is generally called 'a Grey'. These have heads whose features are very like what is shown in Fig. 17.1 and they have been referred to as 'our soldiers' by other more human-like entities. Apart from these, there are many other forms of creature becoming manifest on this planet. Some are so bizarre as to make it impossible to rationalize what they are or what they portend. However, that does not prevent us from doing what we have already done with regard to their spacecraft – namely, taking a limited view of the phenomenon so as not to be overwhelmed by its complexity and sheer, to our limited understanding, impossibility.

In the Introduction to his remarkable book *Transformation* Whitley Strieber (1989) argues from his own experiences with the 'visitors' that they are 'a genuine unknown and not an outcome of hallucination or mental illness'. Later on he says:

This is a subtle, complex group of phenomena, causing experience at the very limits of perception and understanding. It suggests to me that there may be quite a real world between thing and thought, moving easily from one to the other – emerging one moment as a full-scale physical reality and slipping the next into the shadows.

Now, if this is so – and I believe that something like it can occur – then how can *Homo sapiens* join this 'college' of space races who have such things at their command unless they are led to experience them, eventually to become convinced by familiarity that such things can and do exist?

The testimony of Strieber in his two books *Communion* (1987) and *Transformation* (1989) indicates that 'they' infiltrated his life and delivered the experiences he underwent in order that he should thereby be able to give them to the world at large. Strieber had the necessary mental strength to meet and eventually understand in some measure the reasons why, to quote him, 'the visitors took me on a fabulous and terrible journey through my fears'. They stripped him bare of all his hidden and suppressed phobias and forced him to confront all his worst nightmares. He concludes his Introduction with these words:

> The visitors are sweeping up from where we buried them under layers of denial and false assurance to deliver what is truly a message from the beyond. There is something more to us and our universe, and it is rich with the potential of the unknown.
>
> It will be incredibly hard for us to achieve real relationship with the visitors. But also, I can tell you from experience that there will be wonder. There will be great wonder.

Already the visitors' goal is being partially achieved, because these two of Strieber's books have been best-sellers and so the message has gone to a large section of the world's population. It is written by an American in English – the nearest thing we have had to a universal language since the Indo-European, of which the purest surviving example is Sanskrit. Thus the entities behind the visitors ensured the message would get the highest degree of dissemination, even if it were not translated.

In this and other ways a subtle and extremely important phase in the development of our civilization is being forced upon us. We cannot but be moved by the subtle ways the visitors arrive and depart and by their abilities with the creation and disappearance of complex forms. They can apparently manifest whenever and wherever they will and can assume the forms that best suit the situation and the purpose of their visits.

Another important contactee is Uri Geller. Like others, Uri was contacted as a young child, but in his case he was given powers that no others seem to possess. I am convinced that his abilities came from the events which took place in December 1949, in the garden of an Arab house in Tel Aviv. He was just

Fig. 17.1 A typical face of a 'Grey' – the dwarf humanoids that are so often seen by contactees.

three years old but he was able to enter the grounds of the house through loose boards in the fence. The peace and tranquillity of the garden had its effect and he awoke from a long sleep near the fish pond. Going on to explore this wonderland, so different from the anxious hurly-burly of life in Israel under the imminent threat of war, he was suddenly confronted by a huge, silent, bowl-shaped object. He became fascinated by this strange aeroplane, and the feeling of peace and beauty that enshrouded him meant that he felt no fear.

As he describes it in *My Story* (1975):

> I had been playing all alone, sometimes dozing and dreaming in the garden during the afternoon. Suddenly there was a very loud, high-pitched ringing in my ears. All other sounds stopped. And it was strange, as if time had suddenly stood still. The trees didn't move in the wind. Something made me look at the sky. I remember it well. There was a silvery mass of light and I even remember the first thought that passed through my head: what happened to the sun?

This was not the sun, and I knew it. The light was too close to me. Then it came down lower, I remember, very close to me. The colour was brilliant. I felt as if I had been knocked over backward. There was a sharp pain in my forehead. Then I was knocked out. I lost consciousness completely. I don't know how long I lay there but when I awoke I rushed home and told my mother. She was angry and worried. Deep down, I knew that something important had happened.

Certainly something of immense importance had happened, because I believe that the most likely explanation for Uri Geller's amazing feats is that a part of his brain that in everyone else lies dormant was programmed by this UFO event. Those entities who wished to use him could then work through him and at the same time affect thousands of others, just as a TV company will work through the medium of millions of TV sets to influence in certain ways a vast number of people.

The purpose of Geller's demonstrations, I believe, is, as far as the programming entities are concerned, to make it appear more possible to a very wide spectrum of people that the examples of psychokinesis, teletransportation of objects and their sudden vanishings (as described in Puharich, 1974) could be accepted as a fact. In this way, when in the future humans meet other space entities with these abilities, they will not be totally thrown. They will have seen them before, even if they have no idea of how they can be.

As an example of proof for the idea that the 'brainwaves' of one person can trigger similar abilities in others, with distance apparently being immaterial, we can again cite Geller's *My Story* (1975). In a chapter entitled 'It Happens Every Day', Geller explains how he co-operated with the *Sunday People* newspaper in a demonstration of starting clocks and watches and the mass bending or breaking of metal objects that its readers were asked to hold at 12.30 p.m. on Sunday, 25 November 1973. They were asked to stroke the objects lightly with thumbs and fingers.

Geller himself was at Orly Airport, preparing to return to Britain. He began concentrating at 12.15 and then at 12.30 he shouted, 'Bend!' The result was that the *Sunday People* received over 1,000 letters detailing clocks and watches that had started and forks and spoons that had either bent or broken. The final tally was 1,031 clocks and watches restarted, 293 forks and spoons bent or broken and fifty-one other objects bent or broken.

Among odd things that were triggered by Geller's intervention we find a watch in Birmingham that started up but went backwards, a watch in Dorset that had not run for forty years starting and somewhere else the bars of a birdcage were bent.

Previously on the *Jimmy Young Show* Geller had done much the same thing over the radio, with results that covered the whole of the British Isles. Geller himself puts it like this:

> I thought that, if people really wanted things to happen in their homes and really concentrated, I could trigger it, because what I do could serve to release the same strange energy in other people. But I was still astounded that so many calls had come from so many places. The BBC switchboard was absolutely jammed.

Next day Geller did much the same thing on TV, and thereby came into contact with the mathematician Professor John Taylor, who eventually managed to get a paper on his experiments with Geller published in *Nature*.

Uri Geller is undoubtedly a phenonemon, but not a natural phenonemon. His powers may lie dormant in all of us, but until the vital centres of our minds are awoken, we cannot do what he can do. He was chosen to deliver a message – to plant ideas in the minds of earth dwellers on which they could mull for the next umpteen years, until such time as some of us at least are fit to join the 'Space Federation'.

A most vital influence over Uri Geller was the neurologist Dr Andrija Puharich, who in 1970 came as a sceptic from the United States to study Geller but ended up being part of the whole amazing Geller saga. It would have been better for Puharich's professional reputation if he had never met Geller, but it is evident from his writings that he became inextricably woven into the pattern of super-normal events that occurred when he began his attempts to record and make sense of the incredible things that were happening under Uri Geller's 'spell'.

We cannot go too deeply into these things and the reader will have to read *My Story* (Geller, 1975) and *Uri* (Puharich, 1974) to reach their own conclusions. However, I believe that Puharich is not seeking cheap publicity when he describes how, for example, his camera case was teleported from where he had left it in New York before flying to Israel to see Geller; however, it was not vouchsafed to him but appeared in Uri Geller's apartment. Nor do I think he is lying when he describes how the tape-recordings he would like to have made were rendered nul and void by the total disappearance into thin air of the cassettes when still in the machine. Or at other times when a message was automatically recorded on the machine although it was not switched on.

Similar events are recorded in Matthew Manning's *The Link* (1987), where items of furniture disappear from one room and are found in another or in the basement. In that case, the medium of communication appeared to be psychic, but we are learning from the developing testimony of contactees that it is often going to be difficult to tell the difference. It also appears that these entities can use any of our modern media devices to transmit their messages. However impossible it may appear to us, it has to be conceded that such things can and do happen, and again this would seem to be part of the teaching process to which we are being subjected. We may either learn or we can hide our heads in the sand and refuse to notice what is happening in our midst.

Puharich has been deeply affected by his experiences in the Geller fold. The voice which was recorded on the otherwise inert tape-recorder had the mechanical quality of synthesized speech – as has been noted in other similar communications from aliens. Thus when the Hindu sage Dr Vinod becomes the mouthpiece for the entities calling themselves The Nine or M, he speaks in a sonorous tone that is not his own. The communicator from The Nine describes them as 'computers', which is probably a vastly too simplistic description but one his recipients could understand.

At one stage Puharich gives his considered thoughts about what he called 'the greater mysteries'. He wonders, as so many others have done, how the Bible can say that God spoke to someone or someone spoke to God. He assumes that beings such as the ones who had contacted him would be even more superior to the people of biblical times and would therefore be God or the gods (*Elohim* in the Bible). A Uri Geller in the time of the Prophets would have been honoured as a prophet, unlike today, when he is treated as a freak or a scientific guinea pig.

Puharich thinks that much can be explained if we identify a local cosmic being of superior intelligence who has been assigned by an even more superior being to a task on earth. Somehow, he says, the cosmic being has control of 'inergy' (short for intelligent energy), which enables him to create forms in the matter-energy continuum as he desires. This has, according to Puharich, been going on for all of human existence.

The local cosmic 'brain' can imitate any language that will enable it to get its message across. It can dematerialize objects and rematerialize them elsewhere at will, but it may need the intercession of a programmed human brain like Uri Geller's to achieve its purpose.

The cosmic brain does not exist in our four-dimensional framework until it has to communicate or interact with us. Thus Uri becomes an intermediary between a cosmic intelligence and humans. The idea would apply to human-like creatures existing anywhere in the universe.

Thus only when there is meaningful communication between the cosmic brain and humans can any real progress be made, but the former is so advanced compared to the latter that it can only be on the aliens' terms. Today, because of the current suppression of moves towards such communication by the scientific establishment, we are maybe as far from establishing it as we have ever been.

At the end of his philosophical thoughts (which I have paraphrased, also adding some of my own), Puharich has this to say: .

> One of the mysteries of the cosmic being was its use of the biconvex disc shape (the flying saucer) to manifest on earth to man and his instruments. I have no idea why this shape is used. This is a matter for scientific study.

Which is just what this book has set out to do. Puharich maybe confuses two distinctly different kinds of alien spacecraft. The flying saucer is an inverted-saucer shape and is not biconvex. That is an attribute of the vaid, which is, I believe, in a different category, being a craft capable of journeys between planets of the galaxy.

What is important, when it seems that in manifesting to us the cosmic entities could assume any shape and appear and disappear like will-o'-the-wisps, is that they seem to need a machine. They do not appear to be able to traverse space without being transported by a device – the device we see so often and which is called the 'flying saucer'. The fact that the thousands and thousands of sightings of discs always have the same general description is very significant and makes it evident that the space races visiting earth are not so superior that they can manifest like the shape-shifters of fantasy fiction. There is a solid component to their activities and maybe one day in the not too distant future we might conceivably be able to colonize the nearer planets in a similar machine. Then it will no longer appear such a mystery.

Bibliography

Bartholomew, Alick (ed.), *Crop Circles*, Gateway, 1991.

Berlitz, Charles, *The Bermuda Triangle*, Souvenir, 1975.

Blumrich, Josef, *The Spaceships of Ezekiel*, Corgi, 1974.

Bowen, Charles, *The Humanoids*, Spearman, 1969.

Buttlar, Johannes von, *The UFO Phenomenon*, Sidgwick and Jackson, 1979.

Chapman, Robert, *Unidentified Flying Objects*, Arthur Barker, 1969.

Charroux, Robert, *The Mysterious Unknown*, Spearman, 1972.

Collins, Andrew, *The Circlemakers*, ABC Books, 1992.

Cramp, Leonard G., *Space, Gravity and the Flying Saucer*, Werner Laurie, 1954.

Delgado, Pat, and Colin Andrews, *Circular Evidence*, Bloomsbury, 1990.

Drake, Raymond, *Spacemen in the Ancient East*, Spearman, 1968.

Erber, Thomas, 'The Velocity of Light in a Magnetic Field', *Nature*, 1 April 1961.

Fewkes, Jesse Walter, *Designs on Prehistoric Hopi Pottery*, Dover, 1973.

Finch, Bernard, 'The Langenhoe Incident', *Flying Saucer Review*, November–December 1965.

Geller, Uri, *My Story*, Robson Books, 1975.

Glasstone, Samuel, *Sourcebooks on Atomic Energy*, Van Nostrand, 1958.

Good, Timothy (ed.), *The UFO Report 1992*, Sidgwick and Jackson, 1992.

Hawking, Stephen, *A Brief History of Time*, Bantam, 1988.

Hilton, Alan, 'Abduction', *Skylink*, No. 4, 1993 (Highland Glen, Gravesend Road, Shorne, Kent DA12 3JW).

Homet, Marcel, *Sons of the Sun*, Spearman, 1963.

Hopkins, Budd, *Intruders*, Sphere, 1988.

Hynek, J. Alan, *The UFO Experience*, Abelard-Schuman, 1972.

Jessup, M. K., *The 1956 UFO Annual*, Arco, 1956.

Keyhoe, Donald, *The Flying Saucer Conspiracy*, Henry Holt, 1955.

—— *Aliens from Space*, Panther, 1957.

Kinder, Gary, *Light Years*, Viking, 1987.

Landsbury, Alan, *In Search of Extraterrestrials*, Bantam, 1976.

Langford, David (ed.), *William Robert Loosley: An Account of a Meeting with Denizens of Another World, 1871*, David and Charles, 1979.

Leslie, Desmond, and George Adamski, *Flying Saucers Have Landed*, Werner Laurie, 1953.

Lorentzen, Coral and Jim, *UFOs: The Whole Story*, Signet, 1969.

LUFORO Bulletin, 9 January 1962a.

—— May–June 1962b.

Maney, A., *Flying Saucer Review*, Vol. 8, No. 3, 1962.

Manning, Matthew, *The Link*, Colin Smythe, 1987.

Martineau, John, 'Agriglyph Surveys from the 1992 Season' (The Walkmill, Discoed, Presteigne, Powys LD8 2NT).

Michel, Aimé, *The Truth About Flying Saucers*, Robert Hale, 1957.

—— *Flying Saucers and The Straight Line Mystery*, Criterion Books, Inc., 1958.

Michell, John, *The View Over Atlantis*, Sago Press, 1969.

Nubell, Basil, 'The Alex Birch Photograph', *LUFORO Bulletin*, September–October 1962.

Paget, Peter, *The Welsh Triangle*, Panther, 1979.

Puharich, Andrija, *Uri*, W. H. Allen, 1974.

Randles, Jenny, and Paul Whetnall, *Alien Contact*, Spearman, 1981.

Shuttlewood, Arthur, *The Warminster Mystery*, Spearman, 1967,

—— *The Flying Saucerers*, Sphere, 1976.

Strieber, Whitley, *Communion*, Arrow, 1987.

—— *Transformation*, Arrow, 1989.

—— *Majestic*, Macdonald, 1990.

Vallée, Jacques, *Anatomy of a Phenomenon*, Spearman, 1966.

—— *Challenge to Science*, Spearman, 1967.

Watts, Alan, 'Activities over Essex, 30 June/1 July 1961', *LUFORO Bulletin*, January–February 1962.

——'An Experiment on the Effect of an External Magnetic Field on the Ignition Coil of a Car', *BUFORA Journal*, Autumn 1964.

Wilson, Don, *Secrets of Our Spaceship Moon*, Sphere, 1980.

Winnick, Herman, 'Synchrotron Radiation', *Scientific American*, November 1987.

Index